ITALY

UNPACKED

Clive Gifford

Published in 2014 by Wayland
Copyright © Wayland 2014

Wayland
338 Euston Road
London NW1 3BH

Wayland Australia
Level 17/207 Kent Street
Sydney, NSW 2000

Editors: Annabel Stones and Elizabeth Brent
Designer: Peter Clayman
Cover design by Matthew Kelly

Dewey number: 945'.09312-dc23

ISBN 978 0 7502 8401 1

Printed in China

10 9 8 7 6 5 4 3 2 1

Picture acknowledgements: All images, including cover images and graphic
elements, courtesy of Shutterstock except: p5 © Luca Zennaro/epa/Corbis
(br); p7 © 1001nights/iStock (b); p10 © carterdayne/iStock (tl); p11 © Sjo/
iStock (tr), © Bloomberg via Getty images (r); p12 © SerafinoMozzo (br); p13
© igorDutina (tl); p14 © Bloomberg via Getty images (l); p19 © Peter Barritt/
SuperStock/Corbis (tr); p21 © Daniel Dal Zennaro/epa/Corbis (l); p24 ©
Angelafoto/iStock (r), © Angelafoto (l); p25 © Massimo Merlini/iStock (t); p28
© Lifesizeimages/iStock (tl), © Francis G. Mayer/Corbis (tm)

The website addresses (URLs) included in this book were valid at the time of
going to press. However, it is possible that contents or addresses may
change following the publication of this book. No responsibility for any such
changes can be accepted by either the author or the Publisher.

Wayland is a division of Hachette Children's Books, an Hachette UK company.
www.hachette.co.uk

Contents

Italy: Unpacked

Welcome to Italy, a boot-shaped country full of phenomenal history and culture sticking out into the Mediterranean Sea. Once the centre of the Roman Empire, it was the biggest and most powerful ancient civilization the world had ever seen. Italy today is packed full of astonishing art, amazing architecture and spectacular scenery. So, if you want to learn about leaning towers, spy the world's sleekest sports cars and check out some of Europe's most amazing foods and inventions, you've come to the right place!

Fact file

Flag:

Area: 301,340km²
Population: 61.5 million
Capital city: Rome
Land Borders: 1,899.2km with six countries
Currency: The Euro

Useful Phrases

Ciao - Hello (informal)
Grazie tante - Thanks very much
Parlo poco Italiano - I speak a little Italian
Buona giornata - Have a nice day
Scusi, dov'è il bagno? - Excuse me, where's the toilet?
Quale è il suo nome? - What is your name?
Prego - You're welcome
Non capisco - I don't understand

A famous Italian tongue twister is:

"Trentatré trentini entrarono a
Trento tutti e trentatré trotterellando"

Thirty three people from Trento entered
the city, all thirty three waddling!

CITY PASS 1

CITY PASS 2

CITY PASS 3

There is a ban on building sandcastles
on the beaches of Eraclea, near Venice.
You can be fined 250 euros if you get
out your bucket and spade.

In 2008, Vittorio Innocente set a new world record
for cycling underwater, pedalling his bike 66.5m
in the Ligunan Sea close to the city of Genoa.

The Romans

In the 3rd century BCE, the small state of Rome captured its first foreign territory, Sicily, the largest island in the Mediterranean. The next 350 years saw the Romans expand their territory greatly. With a powerful and disciplined army conquering all before them, the Romans built an enormous empire that stretched throughout much of Europe and North Africa. At its largest, it covered an area of 6.5 million km².

The Pont du Gard aqueduct is 275m long and almost 50m high.

Roman Engineering

The Romans were masterful engineers who made great use of the arch and strong concrete. They built a range of structures, from bridges and aqueducts to carry fresh water, to famous buildings like the Pantheon in Rome, that exists to this day. Towns and cities were linked by networks of well-built, straight roads. At the empire's peak, some 400,000km of roads existed, including the Appian Way linking Rome to Brindisi in southeastern Italy. It also encouraged farmers to combine their land, creating larger farms.

Trajan's Forum in Rome was bigger than two soccer pitches.

NO WAY!

Roman feasts featured some outrageous dishes including flamingo tongues, cow udders stuffed with sea urchins and stuffed dormice rolled in honey. Many dishes were covered in garum, a pungent sauce made from rotting fish intestines.

Roman Settlements

Roman cities featured advanced sewage systems, public baths and meeting places and markets. Trajan's Forum in Rome, for example, held spaces for more than 150 shops, and was one of the world's first shopping malls. Many poorer Romans lived in *insulae* apartment buildings whilst wealthier subjects lived in larger *domus* or in countryside villas. Some wealthy homes had mosaic-tiled floors and central heating systems called hypocausts which channelled hot air from a furnace under floors and up walls.

Roman soldiers marched rapidly, up to 35km a day.

Life and Death

The Romans made many medical advances, including performing caesarean section operations to remove a baby safely if there were complications during childbirth. Some of their cures, though, were less successful such as using earwax to soothe bites and mouse brains as toothpaste. The Romans also delighted in bloodthirsty gladiatorial games held in large stadiums called amphitheatres and featuring men battling with wild animals or each other, often to the death.

Rome: The Eternal City

Exciting, chaotic and historic, Italy's capital city is a vibrant tangle of busy streets where modern buildings rub shoulders with ancient art and architecture. As the centre of the mighty Roman Empire, Rome was the most powerful city in the world for 700 years. Today, it remains a major world city attracting more than 7 million visitors a year.

Seven Hills

Rome started out as a crossing over the River Tiber but developed into a large settlement built over seven low-lying hills. By 50 BCE, its population had passed one million. No city would match it in size for over 1,800 years. The Romans left behind awesome structures such as the Colosseum where gladiatorial games were held in front of enormous crowds.

Many of Rome's bridges crossing the Tiber are hundreds of years old.

At night, the Trevi Fountain lights up.

A mouthwatering selection of antipasto starters to a meal.

Dinner Time

The Italians eat a wide range of foods, not just pasta and pizza. Beef and pork dishes are common, as is fish and seafood caught off Italy's 7,600km of coastline. Lunch is often the heaviest meal of the day and consists of a number of courses, starting with small dishes of olives, fish, cheese and meats known as *antipasto*. A common tradition before dinner is to take a leisurely stroll, known as *La Passeggiata*, where you may see neighbours and other people you know also out and about.

Just Desserts

Italians love their desserts, known as *dolce*. These can be as simple as fresh fruit or crispy *biscotti* (biscuits) or complex layered puddings like *tiramisu* or *Zuppa Inglese*. Italian *gelato* (ice cream) comes in hundreds of flavours.

Tasty tubs of gelato. Italy even has a Gelato University near Bologna to teach ice-cream making skills.

La Bella Figura

The Italians believe in a concept called *La Bella Figura* (the beautiful figure). This is not just about how you dress but also about your posture, confidence and politeness in other people's company. Italians don't do saggy trackies, shell suits or onesies. They are amongst the best-dressed people in Europe and the Italian fashion industry is large and influential.

NO WAY!

Famous Italian fashion designer, Giorgio Armani designed the uniforms for the Italian Air Force!

Luxury cashmere clothing is made at the Brunello Cucinelli factory near Perugia.

Major Industry

Fashion, clothing and footwear are major industries in Italy. They directly employ around half a million people all over the country, producing and selling clothes to keep Italians and visitors well-dressed. In 2013, Italy sold approximately 44 billion euros worth of fashion abroad, making it one of the country's biggest exports.

Serie A

One of the greatest leagues in world football, Serie A has long been home to many of the world's best players and clubs. The 20 teams compete from September to May to win the *Scudetto* (shield). Top teams include Napoli, AC Milan, Internazionale (also known as Inter Milan) and Juventus, based in Turin, who have won the league more than any other side.

The mighty San Siro stadium, home to both Inter Milan and their fierce rivals, AC Milan.

AC Milan's Stephan El Shaarawy playing against Inter Milan.

Fans and Derbies

Derby matches between local rivals, such as the derby between Sampdoria and Genoa, especially excite fans. Some great rivals share a stadium, for example, Lazio and Roma both call the Olympic Stadium in Rome their home. Football fans attend games and follow their team's fortunes on the television and the radio. They often play casual games themselves, either full 11-a-side matches or an 8-a-side version of football called *calciotto*.

21

North and South

Italy is a mountainous and hilly country, but that hasn't stopped several million Italians from farming the land. There are over 1.6 million farms and smallholdings in Italy. More than 70% of these are devoted to growing crops. Italian industry is concentrated in the north of the country although oil refineries, chemicals and plastics companies can be found near ports in the south.

Bottles and Bouquets

Many Italian farmers grow wheat, maize or vegetables including tomatoes, soybeans and sugar beet. The warm climate in much of central and southern Italy has allowed it to become one of the world's leading producers of fruits, such as oranges, lemons, peaches and apricots. Many people also grow olives or flowers, and vineyards are found throughout the country.

Around one fifth of all the wine drunk in the world is produced in Italy — that's about 6.6 billion bottles a year!

Palermo

The capital city of Sicily, Palermo was founded almost 2,800 years ago by Phoenician traders. The city has been ruled by many different empires including the Greeks, Normans, Arabs, the Swabians from Germany, the French and the Spanish. Menus in many Palermo restaurants are written out in five or more languages! Palermo is one of Italy's biggest ports, and handles 2 million passengers and around 5 million tonnes of cargo every year.

Naples

Naples is the industrial centre of southern Italy and the country's third largest city. It's perched on a broad bay 190km southeast of Rome, and is home to almost a million inhabitants. The first steam-powered ship in the Mediterranean Sea, the *Ferdinando I*, was launched from the city's dockyards in 1818, and Naples remains a busy port with around a million cruise liner passengers arriving each year. They flock to shop in its many markets and visit its famous old art galleries and theatres, including the Teatro di San Carlo, the oldest working opera house in the world.

NO WAY!

The Capuchin Catacombs in Palermo contain the preserved remains of about 8,000 mummified people, some in lifelike poses. Creepy!

Over 60,000 ships visit the port of Naples every year.

Italian Inventions

There have been plenty of ingenious Italians throughout the ages, but none more so than Leonardo da Vinci (1452-1519). He proved skilled at almost everything he attempted, from drawing, painting and sculpture to engineering and inventing. Da Vinci invented a lens grinding machine whilst also sketching out pioneering plans for ball bearings, armoured tanks, parachutes and a form of helicopter. Here are eight more devices for work and play that were originally developed or invented by Italians.

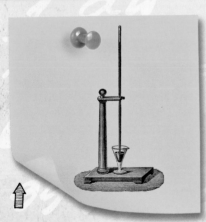

Barometer
Evangelista Torricelli (1643)

This device is used in weather forecasting to measure the pressure of the atmosphere.

Telephone
Antonio Meucci (1860)

The Florence-born Meucci demonstrated his *teletrofono* device in New York, USA, 16 years before Alexander Graham Bell famously made his first phone call.

Electroplating
Luigi Brugnatelli (1805)

The use of electricity to coat metals with a thin layer of gold, silver or another metal. It is used in making jewellery and cutlery.

Space hopper
Aquilino Cosani (1968)

This bouncy ball with handles has given millions of children fun in the garden.

Piano
Bartolomeo Cristofori (1700-1710)

Whilst working in Padua, Cristofori built the first pianos with hammers striking strings.

Commercial espresso coffee machine
Luigi Bezzera (1903)

Bezzera improved existing coffee machines to brew coffee quickly using hot water and steam under pressure.

Radio (practical radio transmissions)
Guglielmo Marconi (1896)

In 1901, Marconi became the first person to send a message via radio waves across the Atlantic Ocean.

NO WAY!

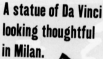

Thousands of pages of notes made by Leonardo da Vinci survive to this day. Most were made in backwards writing, decipherable by using a mirror.

A statue of Da Vinci looking thoughtful in Milan.

Crossword puzzle
Giuseppe Airoldi (1890)

The forerunner of today's crosswords was first published in an Italian magazine.

More information

Websites

- http://www.italia.it/en/home.html
  Italy's official tourism website is packed with information about the country.

- http://www.italiansrus.com/
  Read all about Italian customs and folk tales on this great site.

- http://www.bbcgoodfood.com/content/recipes/cuisines/italian/
  Dozens of mouthwatering recipes for Italian food can be found here.

- http://www.delish.com/recipes/cooking-recipes/italian-recipes
  And more here – from simple *crostini* (toasts with toppings) to delicious desserts.

- http://www.uffizi.com/virtual-tour-uffizi-gallery.asp
  Take a virtual tour of many Italian masterpieces housed at the Uffizi Gallery in Florence.

Apps

Fotopedia Italy A wide and varied selection of groovy photos and facts for your iPhone or iPad.

Italian Lessons and Flashcards Learn some key Italian words and phrases easily with this LangLearner Lessons app for all Android devices.

Mom's Italian Recipes Dozens of tasty recipes from Italy are available using this Android app.

3D Drag Race Start with a Fiat Punto and end up spending your race winnings on a Ferrari or Lamborghini in this simple drag racing game for Android devices.

Movies

Cinema Paradiso (1988) The story of a young boy from Sicily and his love of films and the cinema.

The Italian Job (1969) This classic British film, starring Michael Caine as a gangster trying to steal a haul of gold, is set largely in Turin. It was remade in 2003 with Mark Wahlberg and Charlize Theron.

Il Postino (1994) An exiled Chilean poet moves to a small Italian island and befriends the local postman.

Clips

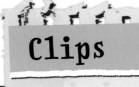

http://www.youtube.com/watch?v=F_wYGcYGXp4
Watch the fast and furiously messy action at the Battle of the Oranges in Ivrea.

http://www.youtube.com/user/LoveSerieA
Catch all the latest Serie A action and highlights on this YouTube channel.

http://www.youtube.com/watch?v=OwpGeXHxo7Q
Let TV historian Adam Hart-Davis guide you through some of the stranger inventions and innovations the Romans brought to Britain.

http://www.youtube.com/watch?v=ATHL-7KfKLO
Watch an epic gondola race taking place in Venice in May 2012.

Books

Discover Countries: Italy by Kelly Davis (Wayland, 2012)

Food and Cooking in Ancient Rome by Clive Gifford (Wayland, 2010)

Leonardo and the Death Machine by Robert J. Harris (HarperCollins Children's, 2011)

The Real: Italy by Paolo Messi (Franklin Watts, 2013)

Rome: An Expanding 3D Guide by Kristyna Litten (Walker, 2012)

A World of Food: Italy by Jane Bingham (Franklin Watts, 2010)

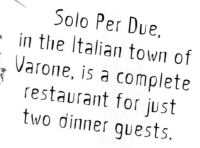

Solo Per Due, in the Italian town of Varone, is a complete restaurant for just two dinner guests.

Glossary

active volcano – A volcano which has erupted recently or is likely to erupt.

Black Death – A plague of disease which struck Europe in the 14th century and killed many millions of people.

commuters – People who travel from one place to another regularly, for example, from home to work and back each day.

decipherable – To be able to solve a code.

dialect – A version of a language spoken by a particular group of people.

exports – Goods or materials which are sent to another country for sale or for trade.

gladiatorial games – Entertainment held during the time of the Romans featuring wild animals and men fighting each other, sometimes to the death.

hydroelectricity – Using moving water to turn machines to generate electricity.

imported – To buy goods or materials in from other countries or regions.

inhabitants – People who live in a place.

manufacturing – Turning raw materials into a finished object or item.

Renaissance – A period of intense activity in the arts, learning and philosophy that began in Italy and spread through Europe in the 14th and 15th centuries.

smallholdings – A term used to describe a small farm, usually run by a single family.

unemployment – To be out of work and without a job.

Index

Nina Börnsen-Holtmann

Italian Design

Benedikt Taschen

PAGE 2 / SEITE 2:
First
Chair, Stuhl, Chaise
Design Michele de Lucchi, 1983
Memphis
H 90 cm, B 69 cm, D 50 cm

ABBREVIATIONS / ABKÜRZUNGEN / ABREVIATIONS:
H height/Höhe/hauteur
L length/Länge/longueur
B breadth/Breite/largeur
D depth/Tiefe/profondeur
Ø diameter/Durchmesser/diamètre

**This book was printed on 100 % chlorine-free bleached
paper in accordance with the TCF-standard**

© 1994 Benedikt Taschen Verlag GmbH
Hohenzollernring 53, D-50672 Köln

Edited by Simone Philippi, Cologne
Design: Mark Thomson, London
English translation: Christina Rathgeber, Berlin
French translation: Thérèse Chatelain-Südkamp, Lohmar
Typesetting: Utesch Satztechnik GmbH, Hamburg
Printed by Printer, Trento

Printed in Italy
ISBN 3-8228-8911-3

Contents

Inhalt

Sommaire

La Linea Italiana

»If other countries had a theory of design, Italy had a philosophy, maybe even an ideology of design«, wrote the Italian semiologist, novelist and cultural critic, Umberto Eco in 1986. His reflection gives some indication of why Italy, and particulary Milan, emerged as the undisputed centre of international design after the Second World War. Beautifully designed Italian products – furniture, lamps, kitchen utensils and cutlery – attracted ever more attention in the western hemisphere during the 1970s and sparked off a veritable fever. Whatever Italy's star designers touched – even such humdrum items as typewriters, can openers or alarm clocks – quickly achieved a status beyond the everyday and became an object with a cultural aura.

The clarity, elegance and distinctive nature of the »linea italiana« – the Italian line – attracted admirers, and the admirers quickly became sworn devotees. Whispering the names of certain lamps or tables to each other like passwords, they knew that they shared the same views and tastes.

Certain Italian radios, televisions, lamps, tables, doorknobs and kettles became cult objects and still enjoy this status – although, of course, every generation creates its own cult objects.

In the 1950s the *Vespa* was so closely associated with a particularly Italian »joie de vivre« that it played a leading role alongside Audrey Hepburn and Gregory Peck in the film, »Roman Holiday« (1953). In the 1960s people were smitten by the new types of radios and televisions manufactured by Brionvega, for compared to the staid wooden boxes of other companies they looked incredibly modern. In the 1970s people raved about Italy's Pop furniture, some of the lamps created by its designers, and Ettore Sottsass' Olivetti type-writer, *Valentine* (1969). The latter was meant to be used less for typing than as a desk-top ornament which signalled that its owner was an intellectual and a Bohemian.

The 1970s and 1980s were the years of the Alchimia and Memphis fevers. Trendsetters who could afford the prices, furnished entire apartments with these pieces. Bold and unconventional, the furniture seemed full of childlike high spirits. Yet there would also be initial enthusiasts – figures such as the German-French fashion designer Karl Lagerfeld – for whom the charm of the furniture wore off after a few years

»Wenn andere Länder eine Designtheorie hatten, hatte Italien eine Designphilosophie, vielleicht sogar eine -ideologie«, schrieb 1986 der italienische Semiotiker, Schriftsteller und Kulturkritiker Umberto Eco. Dieser Gedanke ist nur ein Versuch, das Phänomen »italienisches Design« zu erklären. Wie wurde Italien, speziell Mailand, nach dem Zweiten Weltkrieg zum unbestrittenen Zentrum, ja zum Mekka des internationalen Designs? Als schöngestaltete italienische Produkte – Möbel, Lampen oder Küchen- und Tischutensilien – in den siebziger Jahren nach aufsehenerregenden Ausstellungen in der westlichen Hemisphäre immer bekannter wurden, entfachten sie ein regelrechtes Fieber. Was immer die italienischen Design-Stars anfaßten – selbst banale Dinge wie Schreibmaschinen, Dosenöffner oder Wecker –, erhob sich bald über den Alltag und avancierte zu Objekten mit kultureller Aura.

Die Klarheit, Eleganz und unverkennbare Eigenart der »linea italiana«, der italienischen Linie, fand schnell eine tiefverschworene Gemeinde, die sich nur noch die Namen bestimmter Lampen oder Tische wie Losungen zuzuraunen brauchte, um sich der gleichen Gesinnung und des gleichen Geschmacks zu vergewissern.

Bestimmte Radios, Fernseher, Lampen, Tische, Türklinken oder Wasserkessel aus italienischer Produktion wurden, waren und sind noch heute Kultobjekte, wobei jede Generation ihre eigenen hatte. Wurde in den fünfziger Jahren die *Vespa* als Ausdruck italienischen Lebensgefühls so verehrt, daß sie neben Audrey Hepburn und Gregory Peck eine Hauptrolle in dem Film »Ein Herz und eine Krone« (Roman Holiday, 1953) spielte, waren die sechziger Jahre vernarrt in die neuartigen Radio- und Fernsehgeräte der Firma Brionvega, die sich neben den braven Holzkästen anderer Produzenten aufregend modern ausnahmen. Die siebziger Jahre schwärmten von den Popmöbeln und bestimmten Lampen der Italiener, von der Olivetti-Schreibmaschine *Valentine* von Ettore Sottsass (1969), die weniger zum Schreiben diente als dazu, einen Schreibtisch zu schmücken und ihren Besitzer als Intellektuellen und Lebenskünstler auszuweisen.

Die siebziger und achtziger Jahre standen ganz im Zeichen des Alchimia- oder Memphis-Fiebers. Trendsetter, die es sich leisten konnten, richteten ganze Wohnungen mit den frechen, unkonventionellen, von einem kindlichen Übermut beseelten Möbelstücken

«Quand d'autres pays avaient une théorie du design, l'Italie, elle, avait une philosophie du design, voire même une idéologie» écrivait en 1986 l'Italien Umberto Eco, critique culturel, écrivain et sémioticien. Cette réflexion explique en partie comment l'Italie, et Milan en particulier, devint après la Seconde Guerre mondiale le centre incontesté, la Mecque pourrait-on dire, du design international. Qu'il s'agisse de voitures, de meubles, de lampes, d'ustensiles de cuisine ou de table, les produits italiens aux formes gracieuses déclenchèrent une véritable fièvre dans l'hémisphère occidental quand ils firent leur apparition dans les années 70. Tout objet portant la griffe des stars italiennes du design – même les choses les plus banales comme une machine à écrire, un ouvre-boîte ou un réveil – sortit bientôt de l'ordinaire et se trouva paré d'une aura culturelle.

Avec sa pureté, son élégance, son originalité, la «linea italiana», la ligne italienne, eut très vite ses inconditionnels qui pour se reconnaître entre eux, n'avaient qu'à se chuchoter le nom d'une lampe ou d'une table en guise de mot de passe.

Certaines radios, télévisions, lampes, tables, poignées de porte ou bouilloires de fabrication italienne ont été, et sont encore, des objets de culte et chaque génération a eu les siens. Dans les années 50, la *Vespa* qui symbolisait l'état d'âme des Italiens fut l'objet d'une telle vénération qu'elle joua le premier rôle aux côtés d'Audrey Hepburn et de Gregory Peck dans le film «Vacances romaines» (Roman Holiday, 1953). En revanche, les milieux à la page des années 60 s'entichèrent des nouveaux appareils de radio et de télévision de la firme Brionvega, qui, en comparaison avec les sinistres caisses en bois des autres fabricants, semblaient venir d'un autre univers. Dans les années 70, on raffolait des meubles pop, de certaines lampes italiennes et de *Valentine,* la machine à écrire Olivetti d'Ettore Sottsass (1969), qui servait moins à écrire qu'à décorer une table de bureau et à démontrer que son propriétaire était un intellectuel et un original.

Les années 70 et les années 80 furent placées sous le signe d'Alchimia et de Memphis. Quand ils en avaient les moyens, les trendsetters aménageaient leur appartement tout entier avec ces meubles non-conventionnels et empreints d'une exubérance . Pourtant, certains finirent par les revendre quelques

UP 5–6 La Mama
Armchair series of polyurethane foam
Sesselserie aus Polyurethan-Schaumstoff
Série de fauteuils en mousse de polyuréthane

Design Gaetano Pesce, 1969
C & B

and who would sell it again. Perhaps it was too childlike, too flashy. The Memphis objects turned the 20th century's categorical imperative for design of »form follows function«, (Louis Henry Sullivan) upside down. »Memphis is like a rock star« was how the proud, twelve-year-old owner of one piece of Memphis furniture put it in her letter to the company.

Designers from Milan have been in demand internationally ever since industry realised that beautifully designed products can be sold more easily and at higher prices than unattractive ones. The Italians are now turning their hand to the styling of Japanese cameras and German, French or Japanese cars. It was certainly not to the detriment of the automobile companies that these designers restyled such quintessential German products as the Mercedes and Volkswagen. The international success of the VW *Golf* (»Rabbit« in the USA), for example, must certainly be attributed to its designer, Giorgio Giugiaro. Even the Neapolitans have forgiven him for daring to improve upon the traditional pasta shapes with a new design – the *Marille* for Voiello – that can soak up even more sauce than the ordinary noodle. The Parisians summoned an Italian architect and designer – Gae Aulenti – to design the Musée d'Orsay and the Museum of Contemporary Art in the Centre Pompidou. The language spoken by Italian designs and products, the signs that they send out, are understood all over the world.

The international character of Italian design can also be seen in the fact that it is not merely the work of Italians. Designers such as Toshiyuki Kita and Shiro Kuramata from Japan, Richard Sapper from Germany and Perry A. King and George Sowden from England are all established names in Milan. Italy's successful lines would be inconceivable without their striking designs.

Many historians and culture critics have pondered the reasons for the discreet but irresistible charm of Italian design. The question has also attracted attention from Italians, but they have approached it with their own unique aplomb. »Quite simply, we are the best,« was how the Italian architect Luigi Caccia Dominioni once summed it up. »We have more imagination, more culture, and we are better mediators between the past and the future. That is why our design is more attractive and in tune with the times

ein, wobei einige, wie der deutsch-französische Modeschöpfer Karl Lagerfeld, sie allerdings einige Jahre später entnervt wieder verkauften. Vielleicht war es des Kindlichen, des Grellen zuviel gewesen. Die Memphis-Objekte stellten den kategorischen Gestaltungs-Imperativ des 20. Jahrhunderts, »form follows function« (Louis Henry Sullivan), auf den Kopf. Ein Memphis-Stuhl war ein Memphis-Stuhl, und der Konsument mußte sehen, wie er darauf saß. »Memphis ist wie ein Rockstar«, schrieb die überglückliche zwölfjährige Besitzerin eines Memphis-Möbels an das Unternehmen.

Designer aus Mailand sind in aller Welt begehrt, seit die Industrie begriffen hat, daß schön gestaltete Produkte sich besser und teurer verkaufen lassen als unansehnliche. Italiener gestalten inzwischen japanische Kameras oder deutsche, französische und japanische Automobile. Daß sie Hand anlegten an so urdeutsche Produkte wie Mercedes- oder VW-Wagen, hat den Automobilkonzernen nicht im mindesten geschadet, im Gegenteil. Der weltweite Erfolg des *Golf* zum Beispiel ist sicher seinem Designer Giorgio Giugiaro zu verdanken. Diesem haben selbst die Neapolitaner verziehen, daß er es wagte, die traditionellen Pastaformen noch durch einen neuen Entwurf – die Marille für den Nudelhersteller Voiello, die noch mehr Soße aufnehmen kann als herkömmliche Nudeln – zu verbessern. Eine italienische Architektin und Designerin – Gae Aulenti – wurde von den Parisern gerufen, um ihr Musée d'Orsay sowie das Museum für Zeitgenössische Kunst im Centre Georges Pompidou zu gestalten. Die Sprache, die italienische Entwürfe und Produkte sprechen, die Zeichen, die sie aussenden, werden auf der ganzen Welt verstanden.

Für die Internationalität italienischen Designs bürgt auch, daß nicht nur Italiener es gestalten. Japaner wie Toshiyuki Kita und Shiro Kuramata, Deutsche wie Richard Sapper, Engländer wie Perry A. King und George Sowden haben sich in Mailand niedergelassen, und einige ihrer markanten Entwürfe sind aus der Reihe der erfolgreichen Produkte aus Italien nicht fortzudenken.

Über den diskreten, aber unwiderstehlichen Charme italienischen Designs haben sich viele Kulturhistoriker und -kritiker den Kopf zerbrochen, auch Italiener selbst, diese jedoch mit der ihnen eigenen selbstbewußten Gelassenheit. »Wir sind einfach die Besten«,

années plus tard, comme le couturier franco-allemand Karl Lagerfeld qui ne pouvait plus les voir. Peut-être ces meubles étaient-ils quand même trop naïfs, trop voyants. Les objets Memphis renversaient l'impératif formel du XXème siècle, à savoir la forme suit la fonction (Louis Henry Sullivan). Une chaise Memphis était une chaise Memphis et c'était à l'usager de découvrir comment s'y asseoir. «Memphis est comme une star du rock», écrivait à la firme une fillette de douze ans, heureuse propriétaire d'un meuble Memphis.

Depuis que les industriels ont compris que les produits qui flattent l'œil se vendent mieux et plus cher que ceux qui sont inesthétiques, les designers milanais sont recherchés dans le monde entier. Désormais, les Italiens créent les formes des appareils-photos japonais ou bien encore des voitures allemandes, françaises et japonaises. Le fait qu'ils aient mis la main à des produits typiquement germaniques comme la Mercédes ou la Volkswagen n'a causé aucun préjudice à ces groupes automobiles, bien au contraire. La *Golf* par exemple connut un succès mondial grâce à son designer Giorgio Giugiaro, le même qui pour le compte du fabricant de pâtes Voiello, avait osé enrichir les formes traditionnelles des pâtes italiennes d'une nouvelle ébauche – les *Marille* – qui absorbent encore mieux la sauce. Les Napolitains ne lui ont d'ailleurs pas gardé rancune. Les Parisiens, eux, ont bel et bien fait appel à une architecte et conceptrice italienne – Gae Aulenti – pour la réalisation du Musée d'Orsay et du Musée d'Art contemporain au Centre Georges Pompidou. Les produits italiens parlent un langage et émettent des signaux que le monde entier est capable de comprendre.

Une autre preuve de l'internationalité du design italien est qu'il est aussi réalisé par des non-Italiens. Des Japonais comme Toshiyuki Kita et Shiro Kuramata, des Allemands comme Richard Sapper, des Anglais comme Perry A. King et George Sowden se sont fixés à Milan et quelques-unes de leurs réalisations marquantes font désormais partie des produits à succès «made in Italy».

Le charme discret, mais irrésistible, du design italien a déjà donné du fil à retordre à beaucoup d'historiens et de critiques. Même les Italiens se sont creusé la tête à ce sujet tout en gardant cependant la sérénité des gens qui connaissent leur propre valeur. «C'est tout simplement parce que nous sommes les meil-

Casablanca
Room divider, plastic laminate
Raumteiler mit Kunststofflaminat
Claustra avec laminé synthétique

Design Ettore Sottsass, 1981
Memphis
H 140 cm, B 212 cm, D 46 cm

Solaris
Wooden chest of drawers on tubular steel legs
Holzkommode auf Stahlrohr-beinen
Commode en bois à piètement en tube d'acier

Design Shiro Kuramata, 1977
Cappellini
H 155 cm, B 140 cm, D 80 cm

Architettura
Cabinet
Schrank
Armoire

Design Giò Ponti, Piero
Fornasetti, 1951
H 219 cm, B 81 cm, D 39 cm

Coffee Table
Blue glass top with floral inset in
centre, on a bronze frame
Blaue Glasplatte mit
Blumeneinsatz in der Mitte, auf
Bronze-Gestell
Plateau bleu en verre avec
vase intégré au milieu, support
en bronze

Design probably Giò Ponti, 50s
Fontana Arte
H 34,5 cm, Ø 99, 5 cm

than in other countries.« It almost seems as if the Italians are born with certain talents which other nationalities have to acquire through hard work. Eloquent testimonies to a history and a culture that reach far back into the past can be found throughout the country and have shaped a sense of beauty and form. The Italian climate and landscape encourage a sensitivity, spontaneity and a certain insouciance that allow for inventions which are new while still deeply rooted in traditions. Giò Ponti, one of the century's great architects and designers, coined the phrase that Italy had been created half by God and half by architects. »God made the plains, mountains, lakes, rivers and sky, but the profiles of the cathedrals, facades, churches and towers were shaped by architects. In Venice, God created only the water and the sky. The remainder was made by architects.«

Architects also »make« Italian design. For a long time there was no difference in Italy between the training for an industrial designer and that for an architect.

Since architecture is one of the fine arts, the artistic aspect always plays a primary role in architectural designs. Many Italians speak of »poetries« when they want to describe the concepts and characteristics of individual designers. Italian products reflect this variety.

Economic, political and social conditions served to encourage the interest of architects in industrial design after the First World War and even more so after the Second World War. The reasons for this were described in 1971 by Vico Magistretti, one of the great Italian designers of our age. »The specific historical and political situation in Italy made it impossible to deal with the grand topics of a real architectonic culture. If we look closely at the era between 1945 and 1970, we can see that it was full of failures in all areas – from town planning to development planning, from housing construction to the industrialization of the building trade.« According to Magistretti, it was only in the field of industrial design that designers could freely develop their creative and expressive powers. It is more satisfying for the architect to design a small object that will be sold in large numbers than to design one house in which only a few people will live. »For the simple reason that it is chosen by the person who will be using it, an object has great potential to exert an influence upon the individual. While it might

30. Beaucoup d'objets qui nous surprennent aujourd'hui encore par leur fraîcheur et leur modernité
datent de cette époque. Parmi les concepteurs qui
continuèrent à jouer un rôle après la Seconde Guerre
mondiale, nombreux sont ceux qui avaient déjà
effectué un travail de pionnier dans les années 30.
Citons entre autres Giò Ponti, Marcello Nizzoli, Franco
Albini et Carlo Mollino. C'est au cours de ces années
que des designers plus jeunes comme les frères
Castiglioni et Marco Zanuso présentèrent leurs premières réalisations. Dans les années 20 et 30, furent
créés plusieurs instruments importants de promotion
et de diffusion du design italien. C'est ainsi qu'en 1928,
Giò Ponti fonda sa revue Domus qui aujourd'hui
encore est considérée comme l'un des principaux
porte-parole du design. C'est également dans les
années 30 que la Triennale gagna en importance.
Créée sous forme de Biennale à Monza, elle fut
transférée à Milan au début des années 30. A cette
époque, la ville de Milan était devenue pour l'Italie le
centre de la finance, de l'industrie et des arts –
remplissant ainsi les conditions nécessaires pour
devenir un forum des courants artistiques et culturels.
Les importants groupes industriels, créés au début de
ce siècle, furent la pierre angulaire de nombreuses
réalisations. Des firmes comme Fiat, Lancia et Alfa
Romeo ainsi que le fabricant de machines à écrire
Olivetti s'aperçurent très tôt que la forme du produit
pouvait représenter un argument décisif dans la lutte
acharnée des concurrents internationaux. Depuis le
moment de sa création en 1908 et surtout à partir du
moment où le fils du fondateur, Adriano Olivetti, se
chargea de la direction des affaires, Olivetti laissa ses
designers/architectes s'occuper non seulement de la
forme des produits, mais aussi de l'apparence des
ateliers, de la décoration intérieure et de la publicité.

Sur le chapitre des nouvelles méthodes de production, l'Amérique était le modèle à suivre. Aussi bien
Adriano Olivetti que Giovanni Agnelli, le directeur de
Fiat, s'étaient déjà informés au début du siècle de ces
nouvelles méthodes de fabrication en série qui, exi-
geant une standardisation et une simplification,
avaient par conséquent une forte influence sur
l'esthétique du produit. C'est en 1939 que la *Fiat 508 C*
fut lancée sur le marché. Réalisée par l'ingénieur
Dante Giacosa, cette petite auto d'une simplicité
extrême présentait une ligne harmonieuse et

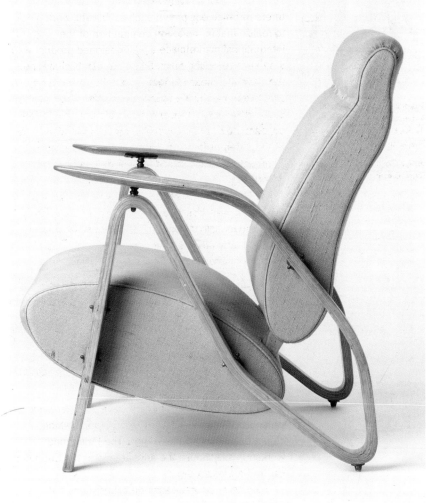

Poltrona con Braccioli Ricurvi
Armchair with curved armrests
Sessel mit geschwungenen
Armlehnen
Fauteuil avec accoudoirs incurvés

Design Carlo Mollino, c. 1952
Apelli & Varesio

popular entertainment medium – which were far ahead of their time. In 1939 Luigi Caccia Dominioni worked out a design with Livio and Pier Giacomo Castiglioni for a Bakelite radio that resembled a telephone and already had some of the character of an electrical appliance. It was manufactured by the Phonola company. Even more functional and significant for the future was an idea which Franco Albini had in 1933, when he simply placed the mechanics of a radio between two sheets of acrylic. Although this set – which still seems modern today – never went into production, it has often been cited as an example of great foresight on the part of a designer.

Modern design emerged out of the close collaboration between the architect Pietro Chiesa and the Fontana Arte company in the 1930s. Chiesa was to become the company's artistic director in 1933. Several of his designs have stood the test of time. His *Luminator* lamp of 1936 is a simple tube that opens into a funnel at the top and emits soft, indirect light. Still in production are Chiesa's crystal table, *2633*, his glass vase resembling a folded serviette and Ponti's lamp, *0024*. During these early days of modern Italian design there was another lamp named *Luminator* that made history. It has been in production since 1929. This lighting appliance, designed by Luciano Baldessari in 1926, resembles a modern light sculpture. There are also several tubular steel chairs from the 1930s which are manufactured today as Modernist classics.

This early phase of Italian design would soon be quashed by political developments. After his march on Rome in 1922, Benito Mussolini established a totalitarian state in 1926. His initial sympathy for modernism and functionalism in architecture and design was soon replaced by a preference for a grandiose Neo-Classicism. Italy was becoming increasingly isolated from international developments prior to the Second World War and would only emerge from this isolation with the end of the war.

In 1945 Italy's economy was completely destroyed. Strong incentives for its revival were provided by the implementation of a reconstruction programme and by an enormous desire to catch up on all that had been missed in the material and cultural spheres. Italian architects were conscious of the role that they played in the restoration of their country and its efforts to

gedachtes Auto mit fließender Linienführung. Vom *Topolino* (Mäuschen), wie das putzige Gefährt im Volksmund bald genannt wurde, liefen bei Fiat bis 1948 150 000 Exemplare vom Band.

Eine dynamische moderne Ästhetik gaben die Karosserieschneider Pininfarina dem Lancia-Coupé *Aprilia*, das bereits 1935 auf den Markt gekommen war. Die Karosseriewerkstatt Pininfarina prägt bis heute das Gesicht europäischer Autos.

Zukunftsweisende Entwürfe gelangen italienischen Designern (die sich erst seit den vierziger Jahren so nennen) beim Radio, das in diesen Jahren zu dem populärsten Unterhaltungsmedium wurde. Luigi Caccia Dominioni entwarf mit Livio und Pier Giacomo Castiglioni 1939 ein Bakelitradio, das an ein Telefon erinnerte und bereits Apparatecharakter hatte. Das Radio wurde von der Firma Phonola hergestellt. Noch funktionaler und zukunftsträchtiger war ein Vorschlag von Franco Albini aus dem Jahr 1933, der einfach die technischen Anlagen eines Radios zwischen zwei Plexiglasscheiben montierte. Dieses heute noch modern wirkende Gerät ging nie in Produktion, ist jedoch als Dokument einer weit vorausschauenden Designerphantasie im Gedächtnis geblieben. Modernes Design entstand in den dreißiger Jahren aus der engen Zusammenarbeit zwischen dem Architekten Pietro Chiesa und der Firma Fontana Arte, deren künstlerischer Direktor Chiesa 1933 wurde. Die Zeit überdauert haben seine Lampe *Luminator* von 1936, ein schlichtes Rohr, das sich nach oben zu einem Trichter weitet, aus dem mildes, indirektes Licht strömt. Noch in der Produktion sind Chiesas Kristalltisch *2633*, seine an eine gefaltete Serviette erinnernde Glasvase und Pontis Lampe *0024*. Noch eine andere Lampe mit dem Namen *Luminator* aus der Frühzeit italienischen Designs machte Geschichte und wird seit 1929 produziert: der 1926 von Luciano Baldessari entwickelte Beleuchtungskörper, der wie eine moderne Lichtskulptur wirkt. Auch einige Stahlrohrstühle und -sessel aus den dreißiger Jahren werden heute als moderne Klassiker hergestellt.

Dieser erste Ansatz italienischen Designs wurde durch die politischen Entwicklungen zunächst erstickt. Nach seinem Marsch auf Rom 1922 errichtete Benito Mussolini 1926 einen totalitären Staat. Seine anfängliche Neigung zu Modernität und Funktionalismus in Architektur und Design wich bald einer Vorliebe für

s'adressait à un grand public. Jusqu'en 1948, 150 000 *Topolino* (le souriceau), comme on l'appelait communément, quittèrent les chaînes de montage de Fiat. Le coupé *Lancia Aprilia*, lui, fut sur le marché dès 1935. Il devait son esthétique dynamique et moderne aux carrossiers Pininfarina qui influencèrent jusqu'à aujourd'hui l'aspect de l'automobile européenne.

C'est avec les radios, toujours plus populaires dans les années 40, que les designers italiens (qui ne se nomment ainsi que depuis cette époque) parvinrent à créer des objets résolument modernes. En 1939, Luigi Caccia Dominioni réalisait avec Livio et Pier Giacomo Castiglioni une radio en bakélite dont la forme évoquait celle d'un téléphone et présentait déjà un aspect technique. Elle fut fabriquée par la firme Phonola. Encore plus fonctionnelle et futuriste était la proposition de Franco Albini en 1933 qui avait tout simplement encastré le mécanisme d'une radio entre deux plaques de plexiglas. Cet appareil, qui nous paraît moderne aujourd'hui encore n'a jamais été produit. Pourtant, il est resté dans les esprits comme le témoignage de l'imagination d'un designer en avance sur son temps. Dans les années 30, la collaboration étroite entre Fontana Arte et l'architecte Pietro Chiesa, qui devint en 1933 directeur artistique de cette firme, donna naissance à un design des plus modernes. Fabriquée en 1936, la lampe *Luminator* de Chiesa a survécu à son époque. Cette lampe est un tube tout simple qui, en s'élargissant vers le haut, prend la forme d'un entonnoir et diffuse un éclairage doux et indirect. La table en cristal *2633* de Chiesa, son vase en verre rappelant une serviette repliée ainsi que la lampe *0024* de Ponti sont toujours en production. Datant des débuts du design italien, une autre lampe baptisée *Luminator* est entrée elle aussi dans l'histoire et est fabriquée depuis 1929: il s'agit d'un appareil d'éclairage, d'une sculpture lumineuse devrait-on dire, qui fut dessinée en 1926 par Luciano Baldessari. Certaines chaises et fauteuils en tubes d'acier des années 30 sont également fabriqués de nos jours et sont considérés comme des classiques modernes.

Ce premier envol du design italien fut tout d'abord stoppé par les développements politiques. Après sa marche sur Rome en 1922, Benito Mussolini institua un régime totalitaire en 1926. S'il éprouvait au début un penchant pour la modernité et le fonctionnalisme, il se sentit bientôt attiré par un néo-classicisme pompeux.

Luminator
Upright lamp of steel
Stehlampe aus Stahl
Lampadaire en acier

Design Achille and Pier Giacomo Castiglioni, 1955
Flos
H 245 cm, Ø 50 cm

Sketch for assembling the *Luminator* 1954/55
Skizze zum Aufbau und zu den Bestandteilen des *Luminator* 1954/55
Esquisse du *Luminator* et de ses pièces détachées 1954/55

Foyer of the Milan Triennale, 1951
Light sculpture by Lucio Fontana
The design was meant to
demonstrate the unity of art
and design.

Foyer der Mailänder Triennale von
1951
Design Luciano Baldessari
Leuchtskulptur von Lucio
Fontana
Der Gesamtentwurf sollte die
Einheit von bildender Kunst und
Design demonstrieren.

Foyer de la Triennale de Milan de
1951
Sculpture lumineuse de Lucio
Fontana
L'ensemble de la création
devait démontrer l'unité des arts
décoratifs et du design.

create products that could compete in the international marketplace. In a speech on the tasks facing architecture delivered at a conference in 1946, Ernesto Nathan Rogers, the venerated old master of Italy's architects, first uttered his oft-quoted phrase, »dal cucchiaio alla città« (»from the spoon to the city«).

As early as 1946 the first furniture exhibition was held in Milan's convention hall. Its themes were economy, functionalism, and good taste. Like everything else, furniture now had to be democratic, which meant that it had to be within everyone's reach. In 1947 the Eighth Triennale was opened in the same building and although the furniture on display was meant for the broad public, it also gave craftsmen and architects a chance to show where the good and modern possibilities for the future lay. It was also in 1946 that Pininfarina presented its legendary limousine, *Cisitalia*, an automobile that was to become the post-war symbol of elegant Italian car design. One need only to compare this automobile with the American models that were being built at the same time to understand the inimitable character of the »linea italiania«. Yet another firm presented a product at this time which would enjoy enormous success for years to come. Until the 1930s the Piaggio firm had been involved primarily in airplane construction and had then begun to fit out ships and build railroad cars. Only one year after the war, the first *Vespas* were already leaving the factory. A revolutionary, new, democratic vehicle for the mass market, the *Vespa* would become the symbol of the new, Italian style of life for the post-war generation. One million were sold within the first decade. Faced with a surplus of starting motors for airplanes, the aeronautical engineer, Corradino d'Ascanio had come up with the idea for the scooter. It was also aircraft construction that had given him the idea for the Vespa's completely new type of wheel suspension. Finally, in 1946 Olivetti also came onto the market with the *Lexicon 80* typewriter. Designed by Marcello Nizzoli, it is the first typewriter to be included in the Museum of Modern Art's design collection purely on the basis of its form. The typewriter had the same soft, flowing elegant streamlines as the *Cisitalia* and the *Vespa*. This was only a foretaste of things to come in the 1950s.

Trained as architects and artists, these designers often refused to accommodate key products to the

einen pompösen Neoklassizismus. Italien geriet vor Ausbruch des Zweiten Weltkriegs in eine zunehmende Isolierung von internationalen Entwicklungen, die erst nach dem Krieg wieder aufgebrochen wurde.

1945 war die Wirtschaft Italiens am Boden zerstört. Doch der große kulturelle und materielle Nachholbedarf und der forcierte Wiederaufbau gaben starke Impulse. Die Architekten waren sich der Rolle bewußt, die sie bei der Wiederherstellung des Landes, bei der Anstrengung, dessen Produkte auf dem internationalen Markt wettbewerbsfähig zu machen, spielten. Auf einer Konferenz im Jahr 1946 prägte der verehrte Senior der italienischen Architekten, Ernesto Nathan Rogers, seine vielzitierte Formel »dal cucchiaio alla città« (vom Löffel bis zur Stadt), als er über die Aufgaben der Architekten referierte.

Schon 1946 fand im Mailänder Messegebäude eine erste Möbelausstellung statt mit den Leitmotiven »Wirtschaftlichkeit, Funktionalität, guter Geschmack«. Wie alles, mußten jetzt auch die Möbel »demokratisch« sein, das heißt, für fast jeden erreichbar. 1947 wurde im gleichen Bau die Achte Triennale eröffnet, in deren Mittelpunkt Einrichtungsgegenstände für ein breites Publikum standen, die jedoch zugleich dem Kunsthandwerk und denjenigen Architekten Raum boten, die einen guten, einen modernen Weg in die Zukunft weisen wollten. Ebenfalls 1946 stellte Pininfarina seine legendäre Limousine *Cisitalia* vor, einen Wagen, der in der Nachkriegszeit zum Sinnbild des eleganten italienischen Autodesigns wurde. Ein Vergleich dieses Fahrzeugs mit amerikanischen Autos, die zur gleichen Zeit gebaut wurden, führt die unnachahmliche Eigenart der »linea italiana« vor Augen. Noch einem anderen Unternehmen gelang ein sensationeller, zukunftsweisender Wurf. Bis in die dreißiger Jahre hatte das Unternehmen Piaggio vor allem Flugzeuge, danach Schiffsausrüstungen und Eisenbahnwaggons gebaut. Bereits ein Jahr nach dem Krieg verließen die ersten Exemplare der *Vespa* die Fabrik, eines revolutionär neuen, »demokratischen« Massenfahrzeugs, das für die Nachkriegsgeneration zum Symbol des italienischen Lebensstils werden sollte. Schon zehn Jahre nach dem Start waren eine Million Fahrzeuge verkauft. Ein Überschuß an Anlaßmotoren für Flugzeuge hatte ursprünglich dem Flugzeugingenieur Corradino d'Ascanio die Idee zu diesem Gefährt eingegeben. Aus dem Flugzeugbau leitete er auch die

A la veille de la Seconde Guerre mondiale, l'Italie se trouvait de plus en plus isolée des courants internationaux, isolement dont elle commença seulement à sortir à la fin de la guerre. En 1945, l'économie de l'Italie était anéantie. Toutefois, le besoin de se rattraper sur le plan culturel et matériel ainsi que la nécessité de tout reconstruire très vite servirent d'aiguillon. Les architectes de ce pays étaient conscients du rôle qu'ils jouaient dans la remise à neuf du pays et dans la tentative de rendre les produits italiens compétitifs sur le marché international. C'est au cours d'une conférence en 1946 que le doyen vénéré des architectes italiens, Ernesto Nathan Rogers, lança sa célèbre formule «dal cucchiaio alla città» (de la cuillère à la ville) alors qu'il faisait un exposé sur la mission de l'architecte.

Un premier salon du meuble se déroula en 1946 au parc d'expositions de Milan et avait pour thème «La rentabilité, le fonctionnel et le bon goût». Désormais, les meubles, eux aussi, devaient être «démocratiques», c'est-à-dire accessibles au plus grand nombre. En 1947, la Huitième Triennale ouvrit ses portes au même endroit. Les objets d'ameublement destinés à un vaste public en constituaient la principale attraction. Toutefois, la Triennale offrait également un espace aux artisans d'art et aux architectes qui, avec leurs produits, voulaient indiquer le chemin solide et moderne de l'avenir. C'est également en 1946 que Pininfarina présenta sa limousine légendaire, la *Cisitalia*, qui devint dans les années d'après-guerre le symbole de l'élégance italienne en matière de design automobile. Une comparaison avec les véhicules américains fabriqués à cette époque fait ressortir le caractère spécifique et inimitable de la «linea italiana». La société Piaggo réussit, elle aussi, un coup sensationnel et ouvrit toutes grandes les portes de l'avenir. Jusque dans les années 30, cette entreprise avait surtout construit des avions, puis des équipements maritimes et des wagons de chemin de fer. Or, un an après la guerre, les premiers exemplaires de la *Vespa* quittaient déjà l'usine. Véhicule révolutionnaire et «démocratique», la *Vespa* devait symboliser pour la génération de l'après-guerre le style de vie italien par excellence. Un an après le début de sa production, le nombre d'exemplaires vendus atteignait déjà le million. C'est à partir d'un excédent en démarreurs pour avions que l'ingénieur aéronautique Corradino d'Ascanio eut

taste of the mass market or to succumb to pressures exerted by the manufacturing companies. Depending on their personal preferences and technical expertise, they would suggest innovations on their own initiative and where they thought them to be necessary. They consciously took on a social function as a moral, aesthetic, and cultural force and became mediators between culture and industry. Design was more than simply a question of assigning a form to an object. It was a synthesis of function, production and the cultural context in which an object was created. The Italian designers had a close spiritual bond to the art world. It has often been noted that there is an affinity between the forms evolved by Italian design in the early 1950s and the organic forms found in the sculptures of contemporary artists such as Henry Moore, Hans Arp, Max Bill and Alexander Calder. In the design work of later decades, stylistic elements of Arte Povera, Pop Art or Arte Ciffra can be recognized.

Spurred on − like Germany − with American economic aid, Italy in the 1950s experienced an economic miracle that affected broad segments of its population. The mobile, consumer society determined the way one lived and also influenced design. Electrical household appliances such as refrigerators, sewing machines washing machines, and dishwashers were in great demand and became objects of mass production. Italy's steel industry flourished and new techniques that it developed, such as die-casting, were taken up by designers. Furniture design often made use of the new inexpensive steel and of the latest developments in automobile production. Marco Zanuso and Osvaldo Borsani designed chairs and sofas that had a great deal in common with car seats. Padded with foam rubber, they were adjustable too, thanks to recently developed mechanisms. The new furniture had to be practical and lightweight, capable of being stacked and folded, and adaptable to rapid changes in living conditions.

In 1951 the Ninth Triennale in Milan had a special exhibition devoted to, »Le forme dell'utile« (The Forms of the Useful), and in the subsequent two years questions of industrial aesthetics would be at the centre of Milan's trade fair. On the initiative of Romualdo Borletti − the owner of the Milanese department store, La Rinascente − and with support from major companies, a number of renowned industrial

völlig neue Radaufhängung für die *Vespa* ab. Und Olivetti schließlich war 1946 mit der von Marcello Nizzoli entworfenen *Lexicon 80* auf dem Markt, der ersten Schreibmaschine, die ihrer Form wegen in die Designsammlung des Museum of Modern Art in New York aufgenommen wurde. Sie wies die gleichen weichen, fließenden eleganten Stromlinien auf wie der *Cisitalia* oder die *Vespa*. Dies war nur der Auftakt für die fünfziger Jahre.

Dank ihrer Kompetenz als Architekten und Künstler lehnten die Designer es weitgehend ab, sich bei Schlüsselprodukten dem Geschmack breiter Massen anzupassen oder dem Druck der Unternehmen nachzugeben. Je nach eigenem Geschmack und technischer Einsicht schlugen sie aus eigenem Antrieb dort Neuerungen vor, wo sie ihnen nötig erschienen. Sie übernahmen selbstbewußt eine gesellschaftliche Funktion als moralische, ästhetische, kulturelle Kraft und wurden zu Mittlern zwischen Kultur und Industrie. Design war mehr als die einem Gegenstand übergestülpte Form. Es war eine Synthese aus Funktion und Produktionsbedingungen sowie der kulturellen Situation, in der ein Gegenstand entstand. Die italienischen Designer standen in enger geistiger Verbindung zur bildenden Kunst. Immer wieder ist auf die Verwandtschaft zwischen den Formen des italienischen Designs der frühen fünfziger Jahre und den organischen Formen der Skulpturen zeitgenössischer Künstler wie etwa Henry Moore, Hans Arp, Max Bill oder Alexander Calder hingewiesen worden. In den Arbeiten späterer Jahrzehnte lassen sich Stilelemente der Arte Povera, der Pop Art oder der Arte Ciffra erkennen.

Italien erlebte − mit amerikanischer Wirtschaftshilfe wie Deutschland − in den fünfziger Jahren ein Wirtschaftswunder, das breite Bevölkerungsschichten erreichte. Mobilität und Konsumlust bestimmten das Leben und beeinflußten das Design. Elektrische Haushaltsgeräte wie Nähmaschinen, Kühlschränke, Wasch- und Geschirrspülmaschinen waren begehrt und wurden in Massen produziert. Die italienische Stahlindustrie erlebte ihre Blütezeit, und die Designer nutzten neuentwickelte Verfahren wie die Spritzgußtechnik. Auch bei Möbelentwürfen griffen sie auf den billigen Stahl und auf Neuentwicklungen der Automobilindustrie zurück. Marco Zanuso und Osvaldo Borsani entwarfen Sessel und Sofas, die viele

l'idée de fabriquer ce véhicule. Il emprunta également au domaine de la construction aéronautique le nouveau mode de suspension des roues.

Enfin, Olivetti lança sur le marché en 1946 la machine à écrire *Lexicon 80*, dont le dessin était de Marcello Nizzoli. C'est en raison de sa forme qu'elle fut intégrée à la collection de design du Museum of Modern Art de New York. Elle présentait les mêmes formes douces, fluides et élégantes que la *Cisitalia* ou la *Vespa* et préfigurait déjà les années 50.

Du fait de leurs compétences en tant qu'architectes et artistes, les designers refusaient pour la plupart de se laisser régenter par le goût des masses ou de céder à la pression des entrepreneurs quand il s'agissait de créer des produits-clés. Suivant leur goût et les considérations techniques, ils proposaient de leur propre chef les innovations qui leur semblaient nécessaires. Très sûrs d'eux, ils eurent alors une fonction sociale, véritable puissance morale, esthétique et culturelle, et commencèrent à jouer le rôle de médiateurs entre la culture et l'industrie. Faire du design ne signifiait pas seulement revêtir un objet d'une forme quelconque. Le design était la synthèse de la fonction et des conditions de production ainsi que de la situation culturelle dans laquelle apparaissait l'objet. De par l'esprit, les designers italiens étaient très proches des arts plastiques. On a maintes fois indiqué la parenté qui existe entre les formes du design italien tel qu'il se manifestait au début des années 50 et les formes organiques des sculptures d'artistes contemporains comme celles d'Henry Moore, de Jean Arp, de Max Bill ou bien encore d'Alexander Calder. Les travaux des décennies suivantes recèlent des éléments stylistiques de l'Arte povera, du Pop Art ou de l'Arte Ciffra.

Tout comme l'Allemagne, l'Italie connut dans les années 50 – grâce à l'aide des Américains – son miracle économique dont profitèrent plusieurs couches de la population. Mobilité et consommation devinrent des règles d'or et influencèrent aussi le design. Les appareils électroménagers comme les machines à coudre, les réfrigérateurs, les machines à laver le linge et la vaisselle faisaient l'objet d'une forte demande et étaient fabriqués en série. Les aciéries italiennes entraient dans leur période de vaches grasses et les designers employaient de nouveaux procédés comme la technique du coulage au pistolet.

Vespa
This vehicle was the embodiment of the Italian way of life. It played a starring role with Audrey Hepburn and Gregory Peck in the film »Roman Holiday« (1953).

Dieser Motorroller war die Verkörperung der italienischen Lebensart. In dem Film »Ein Herz und eine Krone« (1953) spielt sie neben Audrey Hepburn und Gregory Peck eine Hauptrolle.

Ce véhicule symbolisait le mode de vie des Italiens. Il joua le premier rôle aux côtés d'Audrey Hepburn et de Gregory Peck dans le film «Vacances romaines» (1953).

Design Corradino d'Ascanio, 1946
Piaggio

Advertisement by the Tecno
company for the armchair *P40*
Werbung der Firma Tecno für den
Sessel *P40*
Publicité de la firme Tecno pour
le fauteuil *P40*

Design Osvaldo Borsani, 1954

designers formed an association in 1953. The journal
»Domus«, which published an international design
yearbook, wrote, »The era of industrial design has
arrived: not only because of the good taste and
aesthetics of industrial products but also because of
its significance for culture and technology, for civilization and tradition, and for the furnishings and building
industry. Above all, however, it is significant for our
country, whose fundamental principle and mission it
always was (and with God's help always will be) to
create things of beauty«. In 1954 La Rinascente (for
which leading designers created entire furniture
collections) established the Compasso d'Oro Prize
(Golden Circle) to be awarded to industrial products
for their outstanding aesthetic quality and their
technical and functional features. Over the following
decades this prize would enjoy great prestige, but
would eventually be discredited by the fact that –
although generally justified in their choice – the elite
designers on the jury tended to award this prize to
each other. Even today, though, the market still takes
note whenever a product has been awarded this prize.

Notwithstanding its rather elitist aesthetic standards,
Italian design did not lose sight of its democratic
bearings. Renowned designers created apartments,
furniture and utensils for an affluent upper middle
class and automobiles, machines, furniture and
appliances for the broader public. In 1956 Dante
Giacosa's new *Fiat 500* came onto the market. It was
sold worldwide and, like the *Vespa*, became a symbol
of the mobility and democratization of the 1950s. The
Olivetti typewriter *Lettera 22*, designed by Marcello
Nizzoli, was the first compact and lightweight portable
typewriter with a cover for transport. It too was
immediately included in the Museum of Modern Art's
design collection, where its design was praised in the
highest terms – (»it casts a spell through the subtle
arrangement of its parts«; it was also awarded the
Compasso d'Oro.

In the mid-1950s, plastics began their success story.
Many designers were immediately interested in this
new material, for it offered new aesthetic qualities and
the chance of mass production. In the following years
the Italians used plastics to create unconventionally
beautiful furniture and household utensils. In the
1950s, the initiative in this area was taken by the
Kartell company, which had only been founded in 1949.

Gemeinsamkeiten mit Autositzen hatten. Sie waren mit Schaumgummi gepolstert und durch neuentwickelte Mechanismen verstellbar. Praktisch, leicht, stapel- und klappbar, flexibel nutzbar mußten die neuen Möbel sein, geeignet für schnelle Veränderungen der Lebensbedingungen.

1951 bot die Neunte Triennale in Mailand eine Sonderausstellung zum Thema »Le forme dell'utile« (Die Formen des Nützlichen), und in den beiden folgenden Jahren stand die Industrieästhetik im Zentrum der Mailänder Handelsmesse. 1953 schlossen sich auf Initiative des Eigentümers des Mailänder Kaufhauses La Rinascente, Romualdo Borletti, und mit Unterstützung führender Konzerne namhafte Industriedesigner zu einem Verband zusammen. Die Zeitschrift »Domus«, die ein internationales Designjahrbuch herausgab, schrieb: »Die Zeit des Industriedesigns ist gekommen, nicht nur wegen des guten Geschmacks und der Ästhetik von Industrieprodukten, sondern auch wegen seiner Bedeutung für Kultur und Technik, für Zivilisation und Tradition, für die Einrichtungs- und Bauindustrie, jedoch vor allem für unser Land, dessen Lebensgrundlage und Berufung es stets war (und mit Gottes Hilfe stets sein wird), Dinge von Schönheit zu schaffen.« 1954 stiftete das Kaufhaus La Rinascente, das sich von führenden Designern ganze Möbelkollektionen entwerfen ließ, den Preis »Compasso d'Oro« (Goldzirkel) für höchste »ästhetische Qualität sowie technische und funktionelle Eigenschaften von Industrieprodukten«. Diese Auszeichnung erlangte in den folgenden Jahrzehnten hohes Ansehen, geriet später jedoch in Mißkredit, da die Elitedesigner in der Jury sich den Preis – meist zu recht übrigens – immer wieder gegenseitig verliehen. Noch heute wird bei jedem Produkt stets vermerkt, wann es diesen Preis gewonnen hat.

Neben seinem eher elitären ästhetischen Anspruch verlor das Design seine demokratische Ausrichtung nicht aus den Augen. Die anerkanntesten Designer gestalteten Wohnungen, Möbel und Gebrauchsgegenstände für eine wohlhabende Bürgerschicht ebenso wie Autos, Maschinen, Möbel und Geräte für breite Massen. 1956 kam der von Dante Giacosa gestaltete neue *Fiat 500* auf den Markt, der weltweit Verbreitung fand und neben der *Vespa* zum Symbol der Mobilität und Demokratisierung der fünfziger Jahre wurde. Für »jedermann« war auch die

L'acier bon marché fut même utilisé pour les meubles et les automobiles. Marco Zanuso et Osvaldo Borsani réalisèrent des fauteuils et des canapés présentant de nombreux points communs avec les sièges de voiture. Ils étaient rembourrés avec de la mousse et dotés d'un mécanisme original permettant de les régler. Les nouveaux meubles devaient absolument être pratiques, légers, empilables, pliables et flexibles dans leur utilisation. En d'autres termes, ils devaient pouvoir s'adapter aux changements rapides des conditions de vie. En 1951, la Neuvième Triennale de Milan proposa un salon spécial sur le thème «Le forme dell'utile» (les formes de l'utile) et l'esthétique industrielle constitua pendant les deux années suivantes le point fort de la foire commerciale de Milan. En 1953, les designers industriels de renom créèrent leur propre association sur l'initiative de Romualdo Borletti, propriétaire du grand magasin milanais La Rinascente, et avec l'aide des principaux groupes industriels. La revue «Domus» qui publiait également un annuaire international du design écrivit à cette occasion: «Voici venu le temps du design industriel et ce, non seulement en raison du bon goût et de l'esthétique des produits industriels, mais aussi en raison de sa signification pour la culture et la technique, pour la civilisation et la tradition, pour l'industrie du meuble et du bâtiment, et surtout en raison de sa signification pour notre pays dont la vocation a toujours été (et continuera d'être avec l'aide de Dieu) de créer des belles choses.» En 1954, le grand magasin La Rinascente, dont les collections de meubles étaient dessinées par des grands designers, créa le prix «Compasso d'Oro» (cercle d'or) pour les «produits industriels de haute qualité esthétique, technique et fonctionnelle». Cette distinction tout à fait prestigieuse durant les décennies suivantes devait finalement sombrer dans le discrédit. En effet, les élites du design qui composaient le jury se la décernaient à tour de rôle – ce qui d'ailleurs était la plupart du temps justifié. Aujourd'hui encore, on indique toujours sur le produit la date à laquelle il a gagné ce prix. En dépit de ses prétentions élitaires en matière d'esthétique, le design ne perdait pas des yeux son orientation démocratique. Les designers les plus appréciés ne se limitaient pas à l'aménagement d'appartements et à la création de meubles et d'objets pour une clientèle aisée, ils concevaient aussi des voitures, des machines, des meubles et des appareils

With their simple, functional forms and clear colours, Kartell's series of household utensils – lemon squeezers, thermos cups, garbage cans – quickly became classics. With their development of completely new shapes in the 1960s, designers were finally able to rid plastics of the stigma of being cheap substitutes and placed them on a par with traditional materials.

At the beginning of the 1960s the Italian economic miracle and the wave of consumerism peaked. The first critical voices within design circles that warned of the potential dangers of working too closely with industry and capitalism still went unheeded. Indeed, in the design of plastic furniture, electronic appliances and lamps, completely new developments were occurring. The late 1960s saw the designs of the two stackable chairs *Selene* (Vico Magistretti 1966) and *4860* (Joe Colombo, 1968). In both their production technique and shape these chairs would serve as models for the future use of plastics in the construction of furniture. Achille and Pier Giacomo Castiglioni (1964) and
Marco Zanuso and Richard Sapper also broke new ground with their designs for the radio and television manufacturer, Brionvega. Their designs – which stressed the technological character of the sets – were to make the company world famous.
Zanuso/Sapper's *TS 502* radio (1964), their *Doney 14* television (1962) – the first transistor, portable Italian television – and Castiglioni's stereophonic radio and record player *RR 126* (1965) had the appearance of technological equipment. They elicited the enthusiasm of a growing group of confirmed devotees in cities all over the world. By the end of the 1960s, Italian designers began to reap international appreciation. They supplanted the prevailing taste in post-war Europe for Scandinavian design, whose traditionally crafted furniture had been in keeping with the consumer's desire for a contented and safe world.

Italian design corresponded more to the ideas of a modern world with its new production methods, new material, new needs, and a new sense of what life was all about. Before man first walked on the moon in 1969, Achille Castiglioni had designed the metal stool *Allunaggio* (Moon Landing, 1966). Displaying the subtle irony typical of his work, with its three splayed metal legs the stool resembled a cross between an exotic insect and a spaceship.

Olivetti-Schreibmaschine *Lettera 22* von Marcello Nizzoli gedacht, die erste kompakte und leichte Reiseschreibmaschine mit einem Deckel für den Transport. Auch sie wurde umgehend mit der Aufnahme in die Designsammlung des New Yorker Museum of Modern Art geehrt, das hymnisch die Gestaltung lobte (»Das Erscheinungsbild wird verzaubert durch eine subtile Anordnung der Teile«), und mit dem Compasso d'Oro ausgezeichnet.

Mitte der fünfziger Jahre begann der Siegeszug des Kunststoffs. Viele Designer zeigten sofort Interesse an diesem neuen Material, das neue ästhetische Qualitäten und die Möglichkeit bot, Massenprodukte herzustellen. Die Italiener schufen in den folgenden Jahren eigenwillig schöne Möbel und Haushaltsgegenstände aus Kunststoff. Die ersten Beispiele in den fünfziger Jahren waren einige simple Haushaltsgegenstände – etwa Zitronenpressen, Thermosbecher, Mülltonnen – des 1949 gegründeten Unternehmens Kartell, die mit ihrer einfachen, funktionellen Form und ihren klaren Farben sehr erfolgreich waren. In den sechziger Jahren gelang es den Gestaltern endgültig, Kunststoffe durch völlig neue Formerfindungen den traditionellen Materialien ebenbürtig zu machen und sie vom Beigeschmack des billigen Ersatzes zu befreien. So sehr waren Ansehen und gestalterische Reife der Designer gestiegen, daß sie ein Material durch ihre Gestaltung adeln konnten.

Zu Beginn der sechziger Jahren erreichten das italienische Wirtschaftswunder und die Konsumwelle einen Höhepunkt. Erste kritische Stimmen, die sich in Designerkreisen erhoben und mahnend auf die Gefahr hinwiesen, der Gestalter könne von Industrie und Kapitalismus zu stark vereinnahmt werden, verhallten noch ungehört. Dafür gelangen gerade bei der Gestaltung von Kunststoffmöbeln, elektronischen Geräten und Lampen völlig neue Erfindungen. Ende der sechziger Jahre entstanden die beiden Stapelstühle *Selene* (Vico Magistretti, 1966) und Modell *4860* (Joe Colombo, 1968), die in ihrer Produktionstechnik und ihrer Form beispielgebend für den zukünftigen Umgang mit Kunststoff beim Möbelbau wurden. Wegweisend waren die Entwürfe, die Achille und Pier Giacomo Castiglioni (1964) sowie Marco Zanuso und Richard Sapper für den Radio- und Fernsehhersteller Brionvega schufen. Mit dem betont technischen Charakter, den sie den Apparaten gaben, machten die

pour le gros du public. En 1956, la nouvelle *Fiat 500*, dessinée par Dante Giacosa, fut lancée sur le marché. Vendue dans le monde entier, elle devint avec la *Vespa* le symbole de la mobilité et de la démocratisation des années 50. Quant à l'Olivetti *Lettera 22* de Marcello Nizzoli, elle s'adressait également au consommateur moyen. Légère et compacte, elle fut la première machine à écrire portative dotée d'un couvercle. Elle eut, elle aussi, l'honneur d'être intégrée à la collection du design du Museum of Modern Art de New York qui fit le panégyrique de sa forme («Son apparence est sublimée par une disposition subtile de ses pièces»). La *Lettera 22* reçut le Compasso d'Oro.

C'est vers le milieu des années 50 que commença la marche triomphale du plastique. Beaucoup de designers manifestèrent tout de suite un vif intérêt envers ce matériau qui tout en présentant de nouvelles qualités esthétiques offrait la possibilité d'une production en série. Pendant les années qui suivirent, ils dessinèrent des meubles et des ustensiles de ménage à la fois beaux et originaux. Un premier exemple dans les années 50 en fut le programme d'ustensiles courants – presse-citrons, gobelets thermos, boîtes à ordures – de l'entreprise Kartell, fondée en 1949. Avec ses formes simples et fonctionnelles ainsi que ses couleurs claires, ce programme devint vite un classique. En découvrant des formes totalement nouvelles, les designers parvinrent, dans les années 60, à hausser le plastique au rang des matériaux traditionnels et à lui faire perdre son arrière-goût d'ersatz bon marché.

Au début des années 60, le miracle économique italien et la vague de consommation avaient atteint leur apogée. Les quelques voix critiques qui commençaient à s'élever des milieux du design et avertissaient du danger que représentait une trop grande emprise de l'industrie et du capitalisme, n'eurent aucun écho. Bien au contraire, ce fut justement dans le design des meubles synthétiques, des appareils électroniques et des lampes que l'on créa des modèles révolutionnaires. C'est ainsi qu'apparurent vers la fin des années 60 deux chaises empilables, la *Selene* (Vico Magistretti, 1966) et la *4860* (Joe Colombo, 1968), dont la technique de production et la forme devaient servir d'exemples pour l'emploi futur du plastique dans la fabrication des meubles. Les créations qu'Achille et Pier Giacomo Castiglioni (1964) ainsi que Marco Zanuso et Richard Sapper réalisaient pour Brionvega,

Lettera 22
Italy's first portable typewriter
Italiens erste tragbare
Schreibmaschine
La première machine à écrire
portative italienne

Design Marcello Nizzoli, 1950
Olivetti

Olivetti Showroom
Olivetti Showroom
Magasin Olivetti

The lamps of the 1960s also emphasized techno-logical and functional aspects. In their combination of function and imagination, designs which are still in demand today – such as *Spider* (Joe Colombo, 1965), *Taccia* (Castiglioni, 1962), *Arco* (Castiglioni, 1962) and others – set the standards for future generations of lamps. They broke through the hitherto established consensus of what a lamp should look like.

With the economic crisis that set in at the end of the 1960s, the mounting generational conflict also broke out. Till then, the field had still been dominated by such established architects and designers of the pre-war era as Giò Ponti, Luciano Baldessari, Franco Albini, and Marcello Nizzoli, as well as figures from the succeeding generation such as the Castiglioni brothers, Vico Magistretti, Marco Zanuso, and Giuseppe Bertone, to name only a few. Their concep-tual world and use of forms were still largely influ-enced by International Modernism and Functionalism. The 1960s saw a new generation graduate from the universities. The realities of the emerging recession meant that very few of these young architects could find work in industry – even if they wanted it. They were not slow to accuse their predecessors of having become far too dependent upon industry and of neglecting the democratic, social and political responsibilities of design. Self-criticism was also heard amongst the established designers. When the journal »Stile Industria« ceased publication for financial reasons in 1963, its editor wrote in the last issue: »Today, the industrial designer is at the centre of a confrontation between the interests of industry and those of culture. There is still a huge gap between them.« In the 1970s, this »generation of grandsons« would eventually force a creative break upon design.

At first, the young designers – who were greatly inspired by the attitudes of the Pop Art movement – gave free rein to their irreverence and irony. In 1969/70 famous, provocative pieces of furniture were created. The chairs of those years, such as *Sacco* (Gatti, Paolini, Teodoro, 1968); *Blow* (De Pas, D'Urbino, Lomazzi, Scolari, 1967) or *Joe* (De Pas, D'Urbino, Lomazzi, 1971) offered unconventional – and not necessarily comfortable – seating. Young people the world over took to these chairs with enthusiasm. The products revealed a perfect command of plastics, an instinct for the »Zeitgeist« and an exuberant creativity

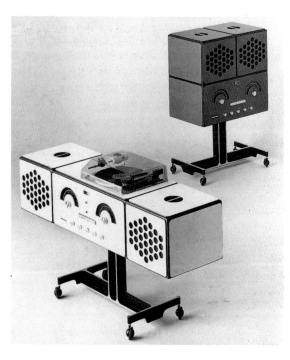

RR 126 Hifi

Stereo system with wooden casing and steel console on castors
Stereokombination mit Holzgehäuse und rollbarer Stahlkonsole
Combiné stéréo avec boîtier en bois et embase roulante en acier

Design Achille and Pier Giacomo Castiglioni, 1965
Brionvega
H 75 cm, B 122 cm, D 36 cm

Designer das Unternehmen weltberühmt. Zanuso/Sappers Radio *TS 502* (1964) oder ihr Fernseher *Doney 14* (1962), der erste mit Transistoren ausgerüstete tragbare italienische Fernseher, Castiglionis Stereoradio und -plattenspieler *RR 126* (1965) hatten das Gesicht technischer Geräte. Sie begeisterten die auf italienische Produkte eingeschworene und wachsende Gemeinde in den Metropolen der Welt. Ende der sechziger Jahre setzte die weltweite Anerkennung der italienischen Designer ein. Sie löste die bis dahin herrschende Vorliebe für das skandinavische Design ab, das in den Nachkriegsjahren mit seinen die Handwerkstradition betonenden Möbeln dem Bedürfnis der europäischen Konsumenten nach Behaglichkeit und einer heilen Welt entgegengekommen war.

Das italienische Design entsprach mehr den Vorstellungen einer modernen Welt mit neuen Produktionsmethoden, neuem Material, neuen Bedürfnissen und einem neuen Lebensgefühl. Noch bevor 1969 der erste Mensch den Mond betreten hatte, entwarf Achille Castiglioni mit der seinen Entwürfen eigenen feinen Ironie 1966 den Metallhocker *Allunaggio* (Mondlandung). Mit seinen drei gespreizten Metallbeinen wirkt er wie die Kreuzung aus einem exotischen Insekt und einer Raumfähre.

Auch bei den Leuchten aus den sechziger Jahren überwog die Betonung des technisch-funktionalen Aspekts. Noch heute begehrte Entwürfe wie *Spider* (Joe Colombo, 1965), *Taccia* (Brüder Castiglioni, 1962), *Arco* (Castiglioni, 1962) und andere setzten Maßstäbe für zukünftige Lampengenerationen durch Funktion und Phantasie. Sie durchbrachen die bisher geltende Übereinkunft, wie eine Leuchte auszusehen habe.

Mit der Ende der sechziger Jahre einsetzenden Wirtschaftskrise brach auch der schwelende Generationenkonflikt offen auf. Bislang hatten noch etablierte Architekten und Designer der Vorkriegszeit wie Giò Ponti, Luciano Baldessari, Franco Albini, Marcello Nizzoli sowie deren Nachfolgegeneration mit den Brüdern Castiglioni, Vico Magistretti, Marco Zanuso, Giuseppe Bertone, um nur einige zu nennen, das Feld beherrscht. Ihre Vorstellungswelt und ihre Formensprache waren weitgehend von der Internationalen Moderne und dem Funktionalismus geprägt. Eine neue Generation verließ in den sechziger Jahren die Universitäten. In der sich bereits abzeichnenden

fabricant de téléviseurs et de radios, étaient elles aussi ultra-modernes et assurèrent au fabricant une célébrité mondiale. Les designers italiens soulignaient le caractère technique de leurs appareils. Qu'il s'agisse de la radio TS 502 (1964) de Zanuso/Sapper, de leur *Doney 14* (1962), premier téléviseur portatif italien doté de transistors, ou du combiné radio-tourne-disques stéréo *RR 126* (1965) de Castiglioni, ils avaient tous une apparence sophistiquée. Les «fans» des produits italiens étaient littéralement enthousiasmés et leur nombre ne cessait de croître dans toutes les métropoles. C'est vers la fin des années 60 que le design italien commença à s'imposer dans le monde entier. Il détrôna le design scandinave qui, en insistant sur la tradition artisanale, répondait dans les années d'après-guerre au désir de bien-être et de sécurité des consommateurs.

Le design italien correspondait plus aux idées que l'on se faisait d'un monde moderne avec ses nouvelles méthodes de production, ses nouveaux matériaux, ses nouveaux besoins et son nouvel état d'âme. Avant même que le premier homme ait mis le pied sur la lune en 1969, Achille Castiglioni réalisait en 1966, avec une ironie subtile que l'on retrouve dans tous ses objets, le tabouret en métal *Allunaggio* (alunissage). Avec ses pieds en métal largement écartés, ce tabouret évoquait à la fois un insecte exotique et un astronef.

Dans les luminaires des années 60, les designers insistaient ici aussi sur l'aspect fonctionnel et technique. Des créations appréciées encore de nos jours, comme par exemple *Spider* (Joe Colombo, 1965), *Taccia* (Castiglioni, 1962) et *Arco* (Castiglioni, 1962), définirent les normes des futures générations de lampes en alliant le fonctionnel à l'original. Elles bouleversèrent les conceptions habituelles que l'on avait d'une lampe et de son apparence.

Vers la fin des années 60, le conflit des générations, qui auparavant n'était que latent, s'exprima ouvertement avec le commencement de la crise économique. Jusqu'ici, les architectes et les designers établis de l'avant-guerre, comme Giò Ponti, Luciano Baldessari, Franco Albini, Marcello Nizzoli ainsi que la génération suivante avec les frères Castiglioni, Vico Magistretti, Marco Zanuso, Giuseppe Bertone, pour n'en citer que quelques-uns, avaient régné en maîtres. Leurs conceptions et leur langage formel étaient fortement

La Sella
Telephone stool, racing saddle, tubular steel bar, cast-iron base
Telefonhocker, Rennsattel, Stahlrohrstange, Fuß aus Gußeisen
Tabouret de téléphone, selle de course, tige en acier tubulaire, socle en fonte

Design Achille and Pier Giacomo Castiglioni, 1957 (1983)
Zanotta
H 71 cm, Ø 33 cm

that still managed to stay within the bounds of »good taste«. Gaetano Pesce, an architect who would come up with his most remarkable designs in the 1980s, gave a first sample of his conceptual world with the swelling forms of his *UP series* of chairs.

Ettore Sottsass Jr, employed during the 1960s as an industrial designer at Olivetti, created his famous fire-engine red *Valentine* typewriter for the company in 1969. Its appearance was meant to signal Olivetti's affinity to Beatnik and Pop culture. This was how the journal »Abitare« described it in 1969: »It is called Valentine and was developed to be used anywhere except the office. It is not meant to remind anyone of the monotonous working day. Instead, it is meant to accompany amateur poets during quiet Sundays in the country or to be a brightly coloured, decorative object on a table in a studio apartment«. The unconventional nature of these designs could hardly be surpassed. It seemed as if an end had been reached.

In the past, the exhibitions at the fairs had often served as a galvanizing influence and provided a taste of things to come, but during these years their subject matter became far less fruitful. Despite a rising unemployment rate and growing economic problems, in 1964 the particularly inappropriate theme of the 13th Triennale was »leisure time«. Although this marked the first time that the environment had attracted attention, the subject was not approached in a critical, analytic manner.

In the autumn of 1969, thousands of workers took to the streets in mass strikes. The young architects supported them, among other reasons because they too felt threatened by unemployment and rejected the system that had precipitated the crisis. As artists, they rejected the techno-functional aesthetics that had long been the nourishing source for the famous elegance of Italian design, seeing it as outdated and little more than empty formalism.

The young rebels formed new groups. While few lasting products would emerge from these groups, their designs, ideas and concepts triggered a new movement and provided important impulses. In 1966, amongst the new groups founded in Florence were the radical architects' groups Superstudio and Archizoom. Concerned with developing an »anti-design« or »radical design«. as well as utopian urban projects, their proposals were widely publicized and elicited a

Rezession konnten nur die wenigsten jungen Architekten eine Arbeit in der Industrie finden – wenn sie es denn gewollt hätten. Sie warfen nun ihren Vorgängern heftig vor, sich zu stark in die Abhängigkeit von der Industrie begeben zu haben und die demokratischen, sozialen und politischen Aufgaben des Designs nicht zu berücksichtigen. Auch bei den Etablierten wurde Selbstkritik laut. Als 1963 die Zeitschrift »Stile Industria« aus wirtschaftlichen Gründen eingestellt wurde, schrieb deren Herausgeber in der letzten Nummer: »Die Position des Industriedesigners steht heute im Mittelpunkt einer Auseinandersetzung zwischen den Interessen der Industrie und denen der Kultur, und noch immer klafft zwischen beiden eine breite Lücke.« Die Enkelgeneration zwang das Design in den siebziger Jahren zu einer schöpferischen Denkpause.

Zunächst ließen die Jungen – stark inspiriert von der Geisteshaltung der Pop Art-Bewegung – ihre Respektlosigkeit und Ironie spielen. 1969/70 entstanden berühmte, provokante Möbelstücke wie die Sessel *Sacco* (Gatti, Paolini, Teodoro, 1968), *Blow* (De Pas, D'Urbino, Lomazzi, Scolari, 1967) oder *Joe* (De Pas, D'Urbino, Lomazzi, 1971), unkonventionelle – nicht unbedingt bequeme – Sitzgelegenheiten, die vor allem junge Leute in aller Welt begeisterten. Die Produkte zeugen vom geschickten Umgang mit Kunststoffen, von Gespür für den »Zeitgeist« und einer überschäumenden Kreativität, die jedoch die Grenzen des »guten Geschmacks« nicht überschritt. Gaetano Pesce, ein Architekt, der vor allem in den achtziger Jahren seine aufsehenerregenden Entwürfe vorlegte, gab mit den schwellenden Formen seiner Sesselserie UP eine erste Probe seiner Ideenwelt.

Ettore Sottsass jr., in den sechziger Jahren als Industriedesigner bei Olivetti angestellt, brachte für den Konzern 1969 seine berühmte feuerwehrrote Schreibmaschine *Valentine* heraus, ein Symbol der Beatnik- und Popkultur. »Sie heißt Valentine und wurde erfunden für den Gebrauch an jedem anderen Ort als einem Büro, um niemanden an monotone Arbeitsstunden zu erinnern, sondern um Amateurdichtern an stillen Sonntagen auf dem Land Gesellschaft zu leisten oder als leuchtendfarbiges Objekt einen Tisch in einer Atelierwohnung zu schmücken«, schrieb die Zeitschrift »Abitare« 1969. Die Unkonventionalität dieser Entwürfe war kaum noch zu

influencés par les Modernes internationaux et le fonctionnalisme. C'est alors qu'apparut dans les années 60 une nouvelle génération sortant tout droit de l'université. En ces temps annonciateurs de récession, rares étaient les jeunes architectes qui trouvaient un emploi dans l'industrie. Encore aurait-il fallu qu'ils le veuillent bien. Ils reprochaient en effet à leurs aînés d'être sous la coupe des industriels et d'oublier les fonctions démocratiques, sociales et politiques du design. De plus en plus de designers établis commencèrent à faire leur «mea culpa». Lorsque pour des raisons économiques la publication de la revue «Stile Industria» fut suspendue en 1963, l'éditeur écrivit dans le dernier numéro: «La profession de designer industriel se trouve au centre d'un conflit entre les intérêts de l'industrie et ceux de la culture que sépare encore un large fossé.» La génération des années 70 s'accorda finalement un répit créatif en matière de design.

S'inspirant fortement de la mentalité du mouvement Pop Art, les jeunes générations laissèrent libre cours à leur insolence et à leur ironie. C'est en 1969/70 qu'apparurent les célèbres meubles provocateurs, comme les fauteuils *Sacco* (Gatti, Paolini, Teodoro, 1968), *Blow* (De Pas, D'Urbino, Lomazzi Scolari, 1967) ou *Joe* (De Pas, D'Urbino, Lomazzi, 1971), des sièges non conformistes et pas toujours confortables qui enthousiasmèrent les jeunes du monde entier. Ces produits témoignaient d'une maîtrise parfaite des matériaux synthétiques, d'un flair particulier pour «l'esprit du temps» et d'une créativité débordante qui restait toujours dans les limites du «bon goût». L'architecte Gaetano Pesce qui défraya la chronique surtout dans les années 80 laissa entrevoir sa philosophie avec les formes généreuses de sa série de fauteuils *UP*.

Ettore Sottsass jr. qui, dans les années 60, travaillait chez Olivetti comme designer industriel sortit en 1969 pour le compte de cette firme sa célèbre machine à écrire rouge tomate, la *Valentine*, dont l'aspect extérieur signalait son appartenance à la culture beatnik et pop. «Elle s'appelle Valentine et a été inventée pour être utilisée partout sauf au bureau. Son but n'est pas d'évoquer la monotonie des heures de bureau mais de tenir compagnie aux poètes amateurs qui courtisent les Muses le dimanche à la campagne ou de décorer une table dans un studio en tant qu'objet de couleur

Taccia
Table lamp of painted metal, glass and plastic
Tischleuchte aus lackiertem Metall, Glas und Kunststoff
Lampe de table en métal laqué, verre et plastique

Design Achille and Pier Giacomo Castiglioni, 1962
Flos
H 54 cm, Ø 49,5 cm

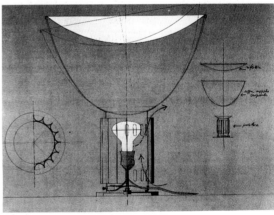

Taccia
Working sketch
Konstruktionsskizze
Esquisse de construction

Quaderna
Furniture series
Möbelserie
Série de meubles

Design Superstudio
(Adolfo Natalini, Piero Frassinelli,
Alessandro and Roberto Magris,
Christiano Toraldo di Francia),
1971

Quaderna
Table, laminated chipboard
Tisch, Spanplatte mit Laminat
Table, aggloméré et laminé

Design Superstudio, 1971
Zanotta
H 72 cm, B 126 cm, D 126 cm

great deal of discussion. The groups brought out several journals and conducted seminars. A few of their designs went into production and were successful. The most famous and long-lasting Superstudio design is the *Quaderna* table (1971) – simple, laconic and elegant, with a latticed, laminated surface. Alessandro Mendini later pointed out that it was especially Archizoom and its leader, Andrea Branzi, that provided a sort of spark for all subsequent developments, from Post-Modernism to Memphis.

In Turin the Strum group was founded; in Venice Gaetano Pesce was developing his archaic-anarchistic designs, and in Milan Alessandro Mendini worked as a designer and as an editor for influential journals which gave a lot of space to the design world's new activities and concerns. Common to all of them was the renunciation of »bel design« and the insistence upon an end or turning point. The »non-realization of one's own designs« was elevated to a programme.

The rebellions only lasted for a few years. In 1972 the Museum of Modern Art held an exhibition that attracted a great deal of attention. Entitled, »Italy: The New Domestic Landscape«, it presented these eccentric designs alongside classic design objects – a clear indication that they were already being seen in historical terms and as manifestations of one particular movement amongst many.

The ongoing discussion, which spread to involve established designers, overshadowed and paralyzed developments in the 1970s. The Compasso d'Oro was not awarded between 1970 and 1979. The oil crisis of 1973 was a further setback to the economy, and particularly for the plastics industry so important to design.

Despite this crisis, and unflustered by the turbulent times, many established designers with close links to industry carried on with their work. Once again this was to be a decade that would produce some of the eventual »classics« and milestones of Italian design. Richard Sapper's *Tizio* lamp, dating from 1972, has remained a top seller for its manufacturer, Artemide, to the present day. In 1986, 15 000 *Tizios* were sold in the USA alone. In 1974 Giorgio Giugiaro's *Golf* rolled off the Volkswagen assembly line. Vico Magistretti's *Atollo* lamp made its first appearance in 1977, and in 1978 Achille Castiglioni's *Cumano* bistro table came onto the market, as did Tomaso Cimini's *Daphine* lamp,

übertreffen. Ein Endpunkt schien hier erreicht.

Die Themenausstellungen der Messen, in der Vergangenheit noch Impulsgeber und Vorreiter, waren wenig ergiebig. Bei steigender Arbeitslosigkeit und wachsenden wirtschaftlichen Problemen war die 13. Triennale 1964 ausgerechnet dem Thema »Freizeit« gewidmet. Wenn dabei auch erstmals das Augenmerk auf das Thema Umwelt gelenkt wurde, so fehlten doch kritische Analysen mit entsprechenden Vorschlägen. 1968 rebellierten auch in Italien die Studenten und Intellektuellen, und im »heißen Herbst« 1969 gingen die Arbeiter bei Massenstreiks zu Tausenden auf die Straßen. Die jungen Architekten ergriffen deren Partei, unter anderem, da auch sie sich von Arbeitslosigkeit bedroht fühlten und das System ablehnten, das diese Krise ausgelöst hatte. Künstlerisch protestierten sie gegen den technofunktionalen Ästhetizismus, aus dessen Geist sich bislang die gerühmte Eleganz italienischer Entwürfe genährt hatte. Die jungen Rebellen schlossen sich zu neuen Gruppierungen zusammen, die zwar nur wenige bleibende Produkte schufen, deren Entwürfe, Ideen und Konzeptionen jedoch eine neue Bewegung auslösten und starke Impulse gaben. 1966 wurden in Florenz neben anderen die radikalen Architektengruppen Superstudio und Archizoom gegründet, die »Anti-Design« oder »radikales Design« und utopische Stadtprojekte entwickelten. Ihre Vorschläge wurden breit publiziert und diskutiert. Sie brachten eigene Zeitschriften heraus und veranstalteten Seminare. Einige ihrer Entwürfe gingen in die Produktion und waren erfolgreich. Der berühmteste und dauerhafteste Superstudio-Entwurf ist der Tisch *Quaderna* (1971), einfach, lakonisch und elegant mit seinem Laminatüberzug im Gittermuster. Vor allem Archizoom mit seinem führenden Kopf Andrea Branzi war, wie Alessandro Mendini später einräumte, eine Art Auslöser für alle späteren Entwicklungen von der Postmoderne bis Memphis.

In Turin entstand die Gruppe Strum. In Venedig arbeitete Gaetano Pesce an seinen archaisch-anarchistischen Entwürfen, und in Mailand wirkte Alessandro Mendini als Designer und Redakteur von tonangebenden Zeitschriften, die den neuen Entwicklungen viel Raum gaben. Ihnen allen gemeinsam war eine Abkehr vom »bel design« und die Beschwörung eines End- oder Wendepunktes. Die

vive«, écrivait la revue «Abitare» en 1969. Il semblait difficile d'aller encore plus loin dans le non-conformisme. Etait-on parvenu à un point extrême?

En automne 1969, les ouvriers descendirent dans les rues et organisèrent des grèves massives. Les jeunes architectes prirent fait et cause pour eux car ils se sentaient d'une part concernés par le chômage et d'autre part refusaient le système politique qui avait déclenché cette crise. Du point de vue artistique, ils rejetaient l'esthétisme techno-fonctionnel, à leurs yeux un formalisme dépassé et creux, bien que l'élégance tant prônée des produits italiens s'en fût jusqu'ici nourrie spirituellement. Ces jeunes rebelles formèrent des nouveaux groupements qui ne dessinèrent que peu d'objets durables. Leurs objets, leurs idées et leurs conceptions devaient toutefois déclencher un nouveau mouvement et servir de moteur.

En 1966, deux groupes d'architectes à tendance radicale furent fondés à Florence, le Superstudio et l'Archizoom, qui développèrent un «anti-design», appelé aussi «design radical», ainsi que des projets d'urbanisme parfaitement utopiques. Leurs propositions furent largement diffusées et abondamment discutées. Ces deux groupes publièrent leur propre revue et organisèrent des séminaires. Quelques-unes de leurs créations furent produites et eurent du succès. La réalisation la plus connue et la plus durable de Superstudio fut *Quaderna* (1971), une table simple, sobre et élégante dont le revêtement en aggloméré montrait un motif de grille. Comme le reconnut plus tard Alessandro Mendini, ce fut surtout Archizoom et son chef de file Andrea Branzi qui jouèrent en quelque sorte le rôle de détonateur pour toutes les réalisations ultérieures des post-modernes jusqu'au groupe Memphis.

A Turin, on voyait apparaître le groupe Strum et à Venise, Gaetano Pesce travaillait sur ses projets archaïques et anarchiques. Enfin à Milan, Alessandro Mendini, designer et rédacteur de revues influentes, accordait une grande importance aux nouveautés en tous genres. Ces designers avaient en commun la volonté d'abandonner le «bel design» et le désir de parvenir à un point extrême ou à un tournant décisif. La «non-réalisation des propres créations» fut érigée en programme.

La révolte ne dura que quelques années. Durant l'exposition spectaculaire de 1972 au Museum of

which proved to be almost as popular as *Tizio*. It seems almost as if the star designers deliberately emphasized classical lines and traditional materials. Mario Bellini designed his *Cab* chair for Cassina – a piece of carefully finished leather was pulled over a steel frame – as well as his classically beautiful *Colonnato* marble table, whose top rests on massive pillars.

In 1981, Ettore Sottsass – a designer of the older generation who had been successful since the 1950s – took stock of the turbulent years. »In the last ten or fifteen years, our work in Italy has been conceptual in nature: we designed very little, few objects and things, few products. Instead, we reflected, wrote, discussed, or drew our opinion on the phenomenon of design and thought about how we could withdraw both ourselves and our designs from the double-edged demands of the capitalist industrial system and, for that matter, of any system… Now, at the end of these… years of debate and general agitation it is my opinion that we did not get very far.«

Sottsass and other designers close to him would be responsible for a new firework of ideas in Italian design. In 1976 the Studio Alchimia had been founded in Milan as a studio for graphic design, and in 1978 it became the centre for the post-radical avant-garde which included figures such as Ettore Sottsass and the young architects, Michele de Lucchi, Andrea Branzi and Alessandro Mendini. Studio Alchimia conceived of itself as a gallery in which unique pieces or prototypes of new furniture would be shown. It was at one of the Alchimia exhibitions in 1978 that Alessandro Mendini showed his *Proust* chair and his *Kandissi* sofa. The first results of his studies of kitsch and the banal, these pieces were followed by his re-designs where he adapted well-known Modernist classics, such as chairs by Marcel Breuer or Gerrit Rietveld.

Sottsass and de Lucchi did not want to be designing prototypes forever. »They did not want furniture for collectors but rather objects that could be sold in stores and used,« wrote Barbara Radice in her chronology of the Memphis movement. Everyone who was involved agrees on December 11, 1980 as the movement's founding day. They met in Sottsass' apartment and listened to Bob Dylan's song »Stuck Inside of Mobile with the Memphis Blues Again«. They chose

»Nichtrealisierung der eigenen Entwürfe« wurde zum Programm erhoben. Die Revolte währte nur wenige Jahre. Eine aufsehenerregende Ausstellung im Museum of Modern Art 1972 mit dem Titel »Italy: The New Domestic Landscape« zeigte diese radikalen und exzentrischen Entwürfe und Konzeptionen inmitten klassischer Designobjekte schon als historisch und gleichberechtigt neben anderen Strömungen.

Die anhaltende Diskussion, die auch auf etablierte Designer übergriff, überschattete und lähmte die Entwicklung in den siebziger Jahren. Von 1970 bis 1979 wurde kein Compasso d'Oro vergeben. Die Ölkrise des Jahres 1973 versetzte der Wirtschaft – vor allem der für das Designgeschäft wichtigen Kunststoffindustrie – einen neuen Rückschlag.

Trotz der Krise und unbeirrt von den Turbulenzen arbeiteten viele etablierte und eng mit der Industrie verknüpfte Entwerfer weiter, und abermals verließ in diesem Jahrzehnt eine Reihe zukünftiger »Klassiker« und Meilensteine des Designs italienische Produktionsstätten. Die Lampe *Tizio* von Richard Sapper entstand 1972 und ist bis heute ein Verkaufsschlager des Herstellers Artemide. 1986 wurden allein in den USA 15 000 *Tizios* verkauft. 1974 lief der *Golf* von Giorgio Giugiaro bei VW vom Band. Achille Castiglionis Bistrotisch *Cumano* kam 1978 heraus, im gleichen Jahr Tomasso Ciminis Lampe *Daphine*, die fast den Verkaufserfolg der *Tizio* erreichte, und 1977 Vico Magistrettis Lampe *Atollo*. Betont, so scheint es, hielten die Stars an den klassischen Linien und traditionellen Materialien fest. Mario Bellini entwarf für Cassina seinen Stuhl *Cab*, bei dem eine sorgfältig verarbeitete Lederhaut über ein Rohrgestell gezogen wird, und seinen klassisch schönen Marmortisch *Colonnato*, dessen Platte auf mächtigen Säulen ruht.

Ettore Sottsass, einer der schon seit den fünfziger Jahren erfolgreichen Designer der älteren Generation, zog 1981 eine Bilanz der unruhigen Jahre: »Wir haben in den letzten zehn oder fünfzehn Jahren in Italien konzeptionell gearbeitet, das heißt, wir haben wenig entworfen, wenige Objekte und Dinge, wenige Produkte, dafür haben wir um so mehr nachgedacht, geschrieben, geplaudert oder die eigene Meinung zum Phänomen Design zeichnerisch formuliert und überlegt, wie man sich selbst und das Design den zweideutigen Voraussetzungen des kapitalistischen Industriesystems oder ebenso jedes anderen Systems

Modern Art, dont le titre était «Italy: The New Domestic Landscape», ces réalisations et conceptions à la fois radicales et excentriques, placées au milieu d'objets plus classiques, étaient déjà présentées comme historiques et de même importance que celles issues des autres courants artistiques.

Les années 70 furent marquées par des discussions qui accaparèrent même les designers établis et paralysèrent par conséquent l'évolution du design. De 1970 à 1979, aucun Compasso d'Oro ne fut décerné. La crise du pétrole de 1973 porta un nouveau coup à l'économie en général et à l'industrie des matières plastiques en particulier, dont l'importance était si grande pour le design.

En dépit de la crise et de tous ces remous, beaucoup de designers associés étroitement à l'industrie continuèrent à travailler, et toute une série d'objets que l'on devait considérer plus tard comme des «classiques» du design sortirent à cette époque des ateliers de production. La lampe *Tizio* de Richard Sapper fit son apparition en 1972. Aujourd'hui encore, elle compte parmi les articles à succès du fabricant Artemide: rien qu'aux Etats-Unis, celui-ci vendit 15 000 *Tizios* en 1986. C'est en 1974 que la *Golf* de Giorgio Giugiaro quitta les chaînes de montage de Volkswagen. La table de bistro *Cumans* d'Achille Castiglioni sortit en 1978 de même que la lampe *Daphine* de Tomasso Cimini, qui fut presque autant vendue que la *Tizio*. Quant à la lampe *Atollo* de Vico Magistretti, elle ne sortit que deux ans plus tard. Il semble que les stars du design aient conservé consciemment les lignes classiques et les matériaux traditionnels. C'est ainsi que Mario Bellini élabora pour Cassina sa chaise *Cab*, un support tubulaire recouvert d'un cuir finement apprêté, et sa belle table en marbre *Colonnato* dont le plateau repose sur un piètement imposant en forme de colonnes.

En 1981, Ettore Sottsass, l'un des designers à succès depuis les années 50, fit le bilan de ces années mouvementées: «Durant ces dix ou quinze dernières années, nous avons travaillé en Italie de façon conceptuelle, j'entends par là que nous avons réalisé peu d'objets, peu de choses et peu de produits, mais qu'en revanche nous avons d'autant plus réfléchi, écrit, discuté, ou formulé notre opinion personnelle sur le phénomène du design. Nous nous sommes également demandés comment nous pourrions nous soustraire,

Total Furnishing Unit
This design by Joe Colombo was included in the environment section of the exhibition »Italy: The New Domestic Landscape«, Museum of Modern Art, New York, 1972.

Dieser Entwurf Joe Colombos wurde 1972 in der Environment-Sektion der Ausstellung »Italy: The New Domestic Landscape« im Museum of Modern Art, New York, ausgestellt.

Cette composition de Joe Colombo fut présentée en 1972 dans le département environnement de l'exposition »Italy: The New Domestic Landscape« du Museum of Modern Art, New York.

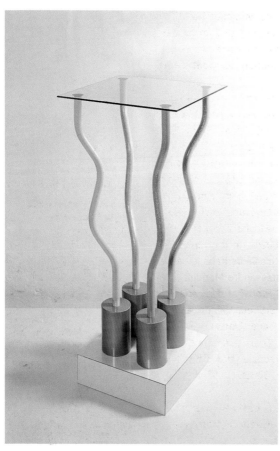

Le strutture tremano
Telephone table of wood, tubular
steel and glass
Telefontisch aus Holz, Stahlrohr
und Glas
Table de téléphone en bois, tube
d'acier et verre

Design Ettore Sottsass, Studio
Alchimia, 1979
H 114 cm, glass top 50 x 50 cm

the name Memphis for their group because it evoked
the blues, Tennessee, rock and roll, suburban America
and ancient Egypt. The group found companies willing
to produce their designs, and the president of
Artemide, Ernesto Gismondi, also became the president of Memphis. The first buyers' exhibition took
place on September 18, 1981 in Milan's Galerie Arc '74
and attracted 2500 visitors. On display were 31 pieces
of furniture, three clocks, ten lamps and eleven
ceramic pieces. People were electrified by this bizarre
furniture in unusual shapes and colours, made of
wildly patterned formica. In only a few years Memphis
was known – and imitated – around the world. Apart
from Sottsass, Mendini and De Lucchi, the group also
included Aldo Cibic, Andrea Branzi, Marco Zanini,
Nathalie du Pasquier, George J. Sowden, Martine
Bedin, and Matteo Thun. The name Memphis became
a byword for a new style, a new culture, a new world
of ideas. Every sort of functionalism seemed to have
been thrown completely overboard. Sottsass declared,
»We… tend to view design as resulting from a series
of coincidences. We imagine a possible complexity
and do not look for what we can leave out. It is our
faith that holds together this tale of coincidences and
gives it a meaning. Every coincidence is given its
formal and decorative identity. A Memphis table is
decoration. Structure and decoration are identical.« De
Lucchi added to this, »design is no longer seen as a
unity but as a sum of parts. We concentrate more on
the elements that determine an object than on the
object itself. Materials and decoration are parts of the
object and as such participate independently in the
design process.« The Memphis objects are strongly
emotional, playful, with a zest for life, amusing, banal
and infectiously optimistic. In the end, however,
Memphis did not produce any furniture of long-lasting
use, but rather objects that conveyed certain
messages. By now, the group has turned towards a
classic, timeless style.

The radical designers did not just achieve a breakthrough for themselves, but also managed to stimulate
the entire design landscape. They liberated the
»beautiful Italian line« from its Sleeping Beauty
existence. Even if the Italian furniture manufacturers
railed against the »unusable, ugly, tasteless Memphis
products«, they all profited from them. As if rain had
fallen after a long drought, design began to flourish all

entziehen könnte... Am Ende dieser... Jahre des Debattierens und der allgemeinen Aufregung glaube ich nun allerdings, daß wir damit nicht sehr weit gekommen sind.«

Sottsass und einige Designer aus seiner Umgebung sollten dem italienischen Design zu einem neuen Feuerwerk an Ideen verhelfen. Schon 1976 war in Mailand das Studio Alchimia als Studio für Grafikdesign gegründet worden. 1978 wurde es zum Zentrum der postradikalen Avantgarde um Ettore Sottsass und die jungen Architekten Michele de Lucchi, Andrea Branzi und Alessandro Mendini. Studio Alchimia hatte das Konzept einer Galerie, in der Unikate oder Prototypen neuer Möbel gezeigt wurden. Im Rahmen der Alchimia-Ausstellungen zeigte Alessandro Mendini 1978 seinen *Proust*-Sessel und sein *Kandissi*-Sofa, die ersten Ergebnisse seiner Untersuchungen über Kitsch und Banales. Ihnen folgten seine Re-Designentwürfe, bei denen er bekannte Klassiker der Moderne wie Stühle von Marcel Breuer oder Gerrit Rietveld umgestaltete.

Sottsass und De Lucchi wollten jedoch auf die Dauer nicht bei Prototypen stehenbleiben. »Sie wollten keine Sammlermöbel, sondern Objekte, die sich im Laden verkaufen ließen und benutzt werden konnten«, schreibt Barbara Radice in ihrer Chronologie der »Memphis«- Bewegung. Als historischer Gründungstag wird von Beteiligten der 11. Dezember 1980 genannt, an dem sie sich in Sottsass' Wohnung trafen und Bob Dylans Song »Stuck Inside of Mobile with the Memphis Blues Again« hörten. Den Namen Memphis wählten sie für ihre Gruppe, weil er an Blues, Tennessee, Rock'n'Roll, an Vorstädte in Amerika erinnert und an Ägypten. Die Gruppe fand Betriebe, die ihre Entwürfe produzieren wollten, und der Präsident von Artemide, Ernesto Gismondi, wurde auch Präsident von »Memphis«. Am 18. September 1981 wurde in der Galerie Arc '74 in Mailand die erste Verkaufsausstellung mit 31 Möbeln, drei Uhren, zehn Lampen und elf Keramiken eröffnet; 2 500 Gäste kamen zur Vernissage. Die bizarren Möbel in ungewöhnlichen Formen und Farben und aus wildgemustertem Resopal elektrisierten die Menschen. Memphis war in wenigen Jahren rund um den Globus bekannt und wurde imitiert. Zur Gruppe gehörten neben Sottsass, Mendini und De Lucchi auch Aldo Cibic, Andrea Branzi, Marco Zanini, Nathalie du Pasquier, George J. Sowden,

nous et le design, aux conditions ambiguës du système industriel capitaliste ou de tout autre système... A la fin de cette... année de débats et d'agitation générale, je crois pourtant que tout cela ne nous a pas menés bien loin.»

Sottsass et quelques designers de son entourage avaient en effet pour mission de transformer le design en nouveau feu d'artifice pétillant d'idées. En 1976, le Studio Alchimia fut déjà créé à Milan en tant que studio de design graphique. Il devint en 1978 le centre de l'avant-garde post-radicale avec Ettore Sottsass et les jeunes architectes Michele de Lucchi, Andrea Branzi et Alessandro Mendini. Le Studio Alchimia était conçu comme une galerie dans laquelle étaient exposés des exemplaires uniques et des prototypes de nouveaux meubles. Ce fut d'ailleurs dans le cadre des expositions Alchimia qu'Alessandro Mendini présenta en 1978 son fauteuil *Proust* et son canapé *Kandissi* qui étaient les premiers résultats de ses recherches sur le kitsch et le banal. Dans les réalisations «re-design» qui leur succédèrent, il donna une nouvelle forme aux célèbres meubles des Modernes, comme les chaises de Marcel Breuer ou de Gerrit Rietveld.

A la longue, Sottsass et De Lucchi ne voulaient plus en rester aux prototypes. «Ils ne voulaient pas de meubles de collectionneurs mais des objets qui pouvaient être vendus en magasins et que l'on pouvait utiliser», écrivit Barbara Radice dans sa chronologie du mouvement Memphis. Le 11 décembre 1980 est cité comme le jour historique de la création de Memphis. C'est ce qu'affirment les personnes qui, ce jour-là, se réunirent chez Sottsass où l'on écouta la chanson de Bob Dylan «Stuck Inside of Mobile with the Memphis Blues Again». Le nom de Memphis fut choisi pour le groupe car il évoquait le blues, le Tennessee, le rock'n'roll, les faubourgs des villes américaines et aussi l'Egypte. Le groupe trouva des entreprises qui acceptèrent de produire ses créations et le président d'Artemide, Ernesto Gismondi, devint également le président de Memphis. Le 18 septembre 1981, la première exposition-vente ouvrit ses portes à la Galerie Arc '74 à Milan. Elle comprenait 31 meubles, trois pendules, dix lampes et onze céramiques. 2500 personnes furent présentes au vernissage. La bizarrerie des meubles en résopal, dont les formes étaient totalement inhabituelles, avait un effet électrisant sur

Murmansk
Fruitbowl, silver
Obstkorb aus Silber
Corbeille de fruits, argent

Design Ettore Sottsass, 1982
Memphis Rossi e Arcandi,
Monticello Conte Otto
H 35 cm, Ø 35 cm

over the country, or, as Sottsass put it, it »exploded like a Nova«. Instead of one or two there were suddenly many movements, from cool High-Tech design to an emphatic Functionalism, from bizarre Post-Modernist outgrowths to luxurious, elegant designs that used the finest materials.

The appeal to the emotions affected the entire design world. While Memphis had made the home into a playground, a comic-strip landscape, other designers turned to »soft« forms and materials, and created swelling sofas (Antonio Citterio: *Sity,* 1986), chairs that offered a safe haven (Gaetano Pesce: *I Feltri*, 1987) or a maximum of relaxation (Vico Magistretti, *Veranda* 1984; Nilo Giocchini/Luca Pettinari, *Itaca*, 1985; Toshiyuki Kita, *Wink*, 1980). There had never been so many original, useful and beautiful lamps developed for a variety of needs in one decade, or such a wide choice of beautiful and functional kitchen utensils and cutlery. Unaffected by the creative excesses of these years, the industrial designer Mario Bellini brusquely observed, »there are no Post-Modern cars. Fiat builds banal cars, but one can use them.« The same applies to computers, offices, chairlifts, telephones, office furnishings and machine tools.

In the 1990s , the variety of design movements reflects the pluralism of a fragmented, specialized society. A fin-de-siècle atmosphere is emerging which leans strongly towards the decorative and makes increasing use of the past. Nevertheless, one can still recognize a few basic features. The rejection of Functionalism and International Modernism means that the right angle is still frowned upon. Curved and swinging lines dominate objects. The legs of tables and chairs are crooked and curving. The swelling padding of the 1950s and 1960s has been surpassed by chairs and sofas with anthropomorphic, female forms. There is a yearning for comfort and safety, for secrets and fairy tales. Lamps with wings and beaks recall mythical creatures and there are beds that look as if they belong in a fairy tale or a dream. It is as if man considers his home a refuge and uses his furniture to decorate a mystic place of worship. The atavistic, archaic appearance of many of these pieces leads one to the assumption that the end of every century demands a look back, a fascinated gaze at the past or at mythic worlds. Furniture as comfort in a world that is becoming ever more difficult to understand? A cause

Martine Bedin, Matteo Thun. Der Name Memphis wurde zum Inbegriff eines neuen Stils, einer neuen Kultur und Vorstellungswelt. Jeder Funktionalismus schien über Bord geworfen. Sottsass erklärte: »Wir … tendieren dazu, das Design als Folge von Zufälligkeiten zu begreifen. Wir stellen uns eine mögliche Komplexität vor und suchen nicht, was man weglassen kann. Unser Glaube hält diese Geschichte der Zufälligkeiten zusammen und gibt ihr eine Bedeutung. Jeder Zufall bekommt seine formale und dekorative Identität. Ein Memphis-Tisch ist Dekoration. Struktur und Dekor sind identisch.« Und De Lucchi ergänzte: »Das Design wird nicht mehr als Einheit, sondern als Summe von Teilen begriffen. Wir konzentrieren uns mehr auf die Elemente, die ein Objekt bestimmen, als auf das Objekt selbst. Materialien und Dekoration sind Teile des Objekts, und als solche nehmen sie am Designprozeß unabhängig teil.« Die Memphis-Objekte sind stark emotional, voller Spieltrieb und Lebensfreude, amüsant, banal und mitreißend optimistisch. Letztlich produzierte Memphis keine auf Dauer brauchbaren Möbel, sondern Objekte, die bestimmte Botschaften übermitteln. Inzwischen hat sich die Gruppe einem klassisch-zeitlosen Stil zugewandt.

Die radikalen Designer schafften nicht nur selbst einen Durchbruch, sondern stimulierten die gesamte Designlandschaft. Sie befreiten die »schöne italienische Linie« aus einem Dornröschenschlaf. Auch wenn die italienische Möbelbranche über die »unbrauchbaren, häßlichen, geschmacklosen Produkte« aus dem Hause Memphis wetterte, profitierten alle von ihnen. Als sei nach langer Dürre Regen gefallen, blühte das Design im ganzen Land auf oder »explodierte wie eine Nova«, wie Sottsass formulierte. Statt einer oder zwei gab es plötzlich viele Strömungen, vom kühlen High-Tech-Design über einen betonten Funktionalismus, über bizarre Ausläufer der Postmoderne bis hin zu luxuriösen, eleganten Entwürfen aus edlen Materialien. Der emotionale Appell griff auf das gesamte Design über. Wo Memphis aus der Wohnung einen Spielplatz, eine Comic-strip-Landschaft gemacht hatte, wandten sich andere Designer »weichen« Formen und Materialien zu, schufen schwellende Sofas (Antonio Citterio: *Sity*, 1986), Sessel, die Geborgenheit (Gaetano Pesce: *I Feltri*, 1987) oder ein Maximum an Entspannung (Vico Magistretti: *Veranda*, 1984; Nilo Giocchini/Luca

les acheteurs. En quelques années, Memphis fut connu sur toute la surface du globe et l'on s'empressa de l'imiter. Outre Sottsass, Mendini et de Lucchi, le groupe comptait également Aldo Cibic, Andrea Branzi, Marco Zanini, Nathalie du Pasquier, George J. Sowden, Martine Bedin et Matteo Thun. Le nom de Memphis devint l'incarnation d'un nouveau style, d'une nouvelle culture, d'un nouvel état d'esprit. Le fonctionnalisme semblait mis au rebut. Sottsass affirma ainsi: «Nous… avons tendance à concevoir le design comme un enchaînement d'impondérables. Nous nous représentons une certaine complexité et ne recherchons pas ce que l'on peut laisser de côté. Nos convictions maintiennent l'histoire de ces impondérables et lui donnent sa signification. Chaque imprévu reçoit son identité formelle et décorative. Une table Memphis est une décoration. La structure et le décor sont des choses identiques.»

Les objets Memphis sont chargés d'émotions, ils manifestent un puissant instinct ludique et débordent de joie de vivre, ils sont amusants, ne sortent pas de l'ordinaire et vous communiquent leur optimisme. En fin de compte, Memphis ne produisit pas de meubles que l'on pouvait utiliser pendant longtemps, mais des objets qui avaient quelque chose à dire. Entre-temps, le groupe s'est tourné vers un style classique et intemporel.

Ces designers radicaux ne créèrent pas seulement une ouverture dans le domaine du design, ils vivifièrent le design tout entier. Ils tirèrent en effet la «belle ligne italienne» de sa torpeur de Belle au Bois dormant. Même si le secteur du meuble fulmina contre ces «produits inutilisables, hideux et dépourvus de goût» venant de chez Memphis, il n'en reste pas moins que tous en profitèrent. Comme si une pluie était tombée après une longue sécheresse, le design fleurit dans tout le pays ou «explosa comme une nova», pour reprendre les termes de Sottsass. Non pas un ni deux, mais toute une série de courants firent leur apparition: du design High-Tech froid et dépouillé aux créations élégantes et luxueuses de matières précieuses en passant par un fonctionnalisme accentué et des courants bizarres, dérivés des Post-modernes.

Cet appel émotionnel gagna tout le design. Là où Memphis avait fait d'un appartement un terrain de jeu, un univers de bandes dessinées, d'autres designers se tournèrent vers la douceur des formes et des maté-

Prototypes of varnished wood for household appliances by Michele de Lucchi. First exhibited at the Milan Triennale in 1979, they never went into production, but did inspire several appliance manufacturers to more cheerful designs: toaster, iron, ventilator, hair dryer, vacuum cleaner, fan heater.

Prototypen aus lackiertem Holz für Haushaltsgeräte von Michele de Lucchi. Sie waren erstmals auf der Triennale 1979 in Mailand zu sehen. Sie sind nie in Produktion gegangen, haben jedoch einige Gerätehersteller zu fröhlicheren Gestaltungen inspiriert: Toaster, Bügeleisen, Ventilator, Fön, Staubsauger, Heizlüfter.

Prototypes en bois laqué pour les appareils ménagers de Michele de Lucchi. C'est à la Triennale de Milan, en 1979, qu'on put les voir pour la première fois. Jamais produits, ils ont pourtant inspiré certains fabricants: grille-pain, fer à repasser, ventilateur, sèche-cheveux, aspirateur, radiateur soufflant.

Philos 33–33 Color
Notebook

Design Michele de Lucchi, 1993
Olivetti
B 27,9 cm, D 21,6 cm, H 4,3 cm

for concern – but there is also the hope that one will be able to rely on the good taste of the Italians. »Tradition is the law of progressiveness,« said the Czech designer Borek Sipek. »Progressive design does not destroy that which was but rather places it in another dimension.«

Pettinari: *Itaca*, 1985; Toshiyuki Kita: *Wink*, 1980) verhießen. Nie waren in einem Jahrzehnt so viele originelle, brauchbare und schöne Lampen für die unterschiedlichsten Bedürfnisse entstanden, eine so große Auswahl an edlen, schönen und funktionalen Küchen- und Tischgeräten. Unberührt blieb von den kreativen Exzessen dieser Jahre das Industriedesign. Mario Bellini sagte barsch: »Es gibt keine postmodernen Autos. Fiat baut Autos, die banal sind, aber man kann sie benutzen.« Das gleiche gilt für Computer, Büros, Sessellifte, Telefone, Büromöbel und Werkzeugmaschinen.

Eine Vielfalt von Designströmungen spiegelt in den neunziger Jahren die Pluralität einer sich zersplitternden, spezialisierenden Gesellschaft wider. Eine Fin-de-siècle-Stimmung breitet sich aus mit zunehmenden Rückgriffen in die Vergangenheit, mit einem starken Hang zum Dekor. Einige Grundzüge zeichnen sich ab: Der rechte Winkel bleibt nach der Abkehr vom Funktionalismus und der Internationalen Moderne verpönt. Geschwungene, schwingende Linien beherrschen die Objekte. Tisch- und Stuhlbeine krümmen und winden sich. Die schwellenden Polsterungen der fünfziger und sechziger Jahre werden übertrumpft durch Sessel und Sofas mit anthropomorphen, femininen Formen. Eine Sehnsucht nach Trost und Geborgenheit, nach Geheimnis und Märchen ist erkennbar. Lampen wie Fabelwesen sind entstanden mit Flügeln und Schnäbeln. Betten erscheinen wie Märchenrequisiten und Traumszenerien. Es sieht aus, als betrachte der Mensch die Wohnung als Fluchtburg, als wolle er mit seinen Möbeln eine mystische Kultstätte dekorieren. Atavistische, archaische Erscheinungsformen legen die Annahme nahe, jedes Jahrhundertende fordere einen Rückblick, ein fasziniertes Starren in die Vergangenheit oder in mythische Welten. Möbel als Trost in einer immer undurchschaubarer werdenden Welt? Sorgen kommen auf, doch auch die Hoffnung, auf den Geschmack der Italiener werde man sich schon verlassen können. »Tradition ist das Gesetz der Progressivität«, hat ein Nichtitaliener, der tschechische Designer Borek Sipek gesagt. »Progressives Design zerstört nicht das, was war, sondern stellt es in eine andere Dimension.«

riaux. Ils créèrent des canapés aux formes généreuses (Antonio Citterio: *Sity*, 1986), des fauteuils pour s'y blottir (Gaetano Pesce: *I Feltri*, 1987) ou pour se relaxer (Vico Magistretti: *Veranda*, 1984; Nilo Giocchini/ Luca Pettinari: *Itaca*, 1985; Toshiyuki Kita: *Wink*, 1980). Jamais ce siècle n'avait vu autant de lampes belles et originales, répondant aux besoins les plus divers, jamais il n'avait vu un si grand choix d'ustensiles de cuisine et de table qui alliaient autant de beauté et de fonctionnalisme. Les excès de ces années-là épargnèrent le design industriel. Mario Bellini dit un jour sur un ton bourru: «Il n'existe pas de voitures post-modernes. Fiat construit des voitures qui sont banales certes, mais que l'on peut utiliser.» Il en allait de même pour les ordinateurs, les bureaux, les télésièges, les téléphones, les meubles de bureau et les machines-outils.

La diversité des courants dans le design des années 90 reflète une société qui s'émiette, qui se spécialise de plus en plus. On ressent une ambiance de fin-de-siècle avec des références au passé toujours plus nombreuses et un penchant prononcé pour le décor. Quelques traits caractéristiques commencent à se dessiner: l'angle droit est toujours banni depuis que l'on s'est détourné du fonctionnalisme et des Modernes internationaux. Les courbes et les lignes élancées régissent les objets. Le piètement des tables et des chaises se cambre et se tord. Le capitonnage rebondi des années 50 et 60 est surpassé par des fauteuils et des canapés aux formes féminines, anthropomorphes. On peut reconnaître un désir de réconfort et de sécurité, une recherche du mystère et du féerique. On a vu apparaître des lampes qui, avec leurs ailes et leurs becs, évoquent des créatures de fable. Les lits semblent sortir d'un conte de fées. L'homme considère son appartement comme une forteresse où il peut se réfugier. Il donne l'impression de vouloir, avec ses meubles, décorer un lieu de culte. Les manifestations ataviques et archaïques font supposer que chaque fin de siècle exige une vue rétrospective, un regard fasciné sur le passé ou sur des univers mythiques. Des meubles pour consoler d'un monde toujours plus impénétrable? Il y a de quoi s'inquiéter. Pourtant, nous avons bon espoir car nous pouvons nous fier au bon goût des Italiens. «La tradition est la loi de la progressivité», a dit un non-Italien, le designer tchèque Borek Sipek. «Le design progressif ne détruit pas ce qui a été mais le place dans une nouvelle dimension.»

Agena
Hanging lamp of hand-crafted glass and metal
Hängelampe aus handgeformtem Glas und Metall
Suspension en verre travaillé à la main et en métal

Design Alessandro Mendini, 1992
Venini
H 42 cm, Ø 48 cm

Beautiful Restraint

Die schöne Nüchternheit

La sobriété dans toute sa splendeur

There are three sources from which Italian design has derived the energy that has made it world famous: an intact structure of small to medium-sized manufacturing companies with highly skilled craftsmen; its design conscious industrial sphere and the creativity of individual, outstanding architects. In the early years of the 20th century the designer did not yet play a distinct role. Furniture manufacturers still designed their furniture themselves. Carlo Bugatti is an example of these Italian »ebenisti« (artist-carpenters), who produced hand-crafted furniture of the highest quality. Unlike his colleagues, Bugatti did not rely solely on traditional models, but also created his own, highly original designs.

During the first decades of the century, automobiles, electrical appliances and office machines began to play increasingly important roles in Western society. This was particularly the case in America, which served as an oft-imitated example. The more progressive Italian industrialists visited America to inform themselves. Yet as early as the 1930s, the Italians were designing their own distinctive automobiles. These were remarkable for their restrained and elegant lines – to the present day this has remained the most important feature of Italian design. A reciprocal relationship between industry and modern art served to stimulate both sides. Futurism, an artistic movement that began in Italy, wanted to lend expression to the dynamism of the modern era and presented this in forceful, avant-gardist pictures and designs.

Great architects – above all, Giò Ponti – designed not only buildings, but also lamps, chairs, tables and glasses, often providing these objects with such practical, perfect forms, that in the 1980s many were once again taken into production. Through his own clear style, his journals »Domus« and »Stile«, and his lectures, Giò Ponti – who detested the superfluous – influenced his own and subsequent generations of architects.

The work of these first »modern« architects and designers in Italy was closely linked to international Modernism, which determined an object's beauty according to its function and material.

Chichibio
Small telephone table, tubular
steel
Telefontischchen, Stahlrohr
Petite table de téléphone, tube
d'acier

Design Giuseppe Pagano
Pogatschnig, Gino Levi-
Montalcini, 1932 (1981)
Zanotta
H 80 cm, Ø 37,5 cm

Interior in Turin
Intérieur à Turin

Design Giuseppe Pagano
Pogatschnig, Gino Levi-
Montalcini, 1931

Follia
Chair of wood and steel
Stuhl aus Holz und Stahl
Chaise en bois et acier

Design Giuseppe Terragni, 1936
(1972)
Zanotta
H 80 cm, B 50 cm, D 60 cm,
Sitzhöhe 41 cm

Follia
Original drawings by Giuseppe
Terragni for the chairs in the
Casa del Fascio, Como, 1932–36

Originalzeichnungen von
Giuseppe Terragni für die Stühle
der Casa del Fascio, Como,
1932–36

Dessins originaux de Giuseppe
Terragni pour les chaises de la
Casa del Fascio, Côme, 1932–36

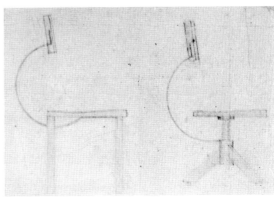

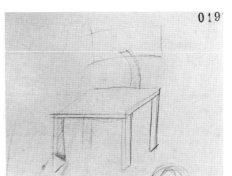

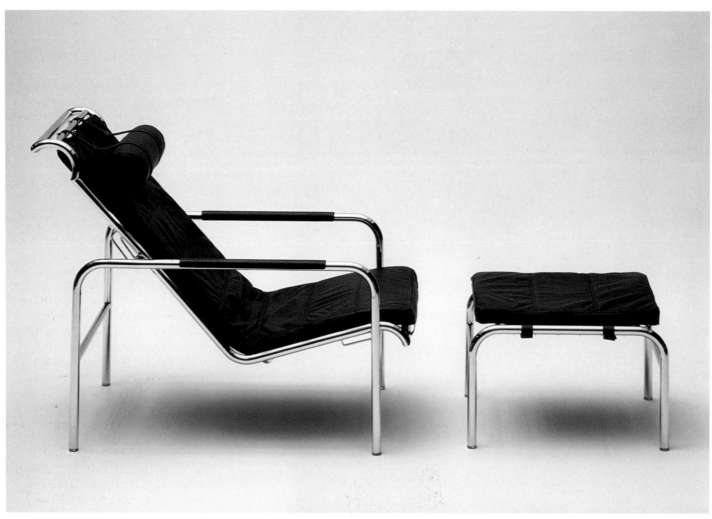

Genni
Couch, tubular steel construction
Liege mit Stahlrohrkonstruktion
Fauteuil de relaxation avec cadre
en tube d'acier

Design Gabriele Mucchi, 1935
(1982)
Zanotta
H 76 cm, B 57 cm, D 109 cm,
Height of seat 41 cm

Genni
Prototype of the couch
Prototyp der Liege
Prototype du fauteuil de
relaxation

Vanity Fair
Leather armchair
Ledersessel
Fauteuil en cuir

Design 1930
Poltrona Frau
H 99 cm, B 96 cm, D 91 cm

Cartocchio (paper bag)
Glass vase
Glasvase
Vase en verre

Design Pietro Chiesa, 1936
Fontana Arte
H 30 cm

2633
Side table of crystal
Beistelltisch aus Kristallglas
Table basse en cristal

Design Pietro Chiesa, 1933
Fontana Arte
H 40 cm, B 70 cm, L 140 cm

Classic pieces of the 1930s were manufactured again in the 1970s and 1980s.
These included Gabriele Mucchi's *Genni*
couch. The Art Déco armchair, *Vanity Fair*
has been in production without interruption
since 1930, as have several designs by
Pietro Chiesa. This architect joined the
Fontana Arte company in 1933 as its artistic
director. The collaboration proved to be
exceptionally prolific. Several of his designs,
such as his *Cartocchio* glass vase, his
crystal table and his *Luminator* have become classics.

Die Produktion erfolgreicher Klassiker aus
den dreißiger Jahren wurde in den siebziger
und achtziger Jahren wiederaufgenommen
wie die der Liege *Genni* von Gabriele
Mucchi. Ohne Unterbrechung wird seit 1930
der Art-Déco-Sessel *Vanity Fair* hergestellt,
ebenso wie einige Entwürfe von Pietro
Chiesa. Der Architekt trat 1933 als künstlerischer Direktor in das Unternehmen
Fontana Arte ein. Die Zusammenarbeit
erwies sich als außerordentlich fruchtbar.
Einige seiner Entwürfe wie seine Glasvase
Cartocchio, sein Kristalltisch und seine
Lampe *Luminator* sind Klassiker geworden.

La production de certains classiques célèbres des années 30, tel le fauteuil *Genni* de
Gabriele Mucchi, fut reprise au cours des
années 70 et 80. Le fauteuil Art Déco
Vanity Fair est fabriqué sans interruption
depuis 1930, de même que certaines
créations de Pietro Chiesa. L'architecte
entra en 1933 comme directeur artistique
dans l'entreprise Fontana Arte. Cette
collaboration s'avéra extrêmement
fructueuse puisque certaines de ses créations, tels son vase de verre *Cartocchio*, sa
table en cristal et sa lampe *Luminatori*, sont
devenus des classiques.

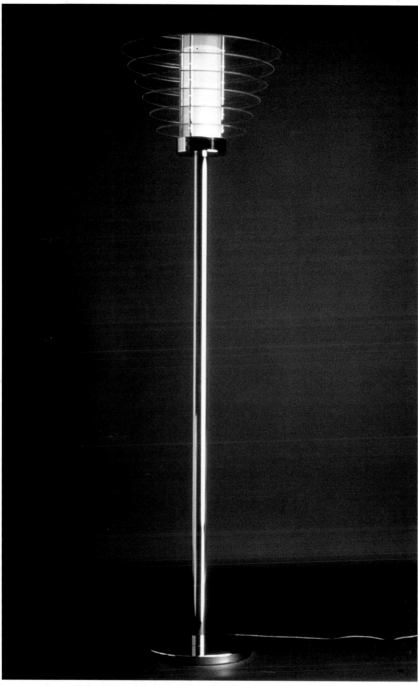

While many of the 1930s designs for lamps and furniture have an utterly timeless clarity, the era's designs for radios and television sets now seem outdated, even though they were considered progressive at the time. The *Phonola* Bakelite radio, which bore strong resemblance to a telephone, was in sharp contrast to contemporary electronic appliances, which were disguised as conservative pieces of furniture. Franco Albini's daring radio design never went into production. Similar ideas would only be taken up again in the 1960s.

Während viele Möbel- und Lampenentwürfe der dreißiger Jahre in ihrer Klarheit absolut zeitlos sind, wirken die Radio- und Fernsehgeräte – die seinerzeit als fortschrittlich galten – überholt. Einem Telefon nachempfunden war das Bakelitradio *Phonola*, das sich bereits erheblich von den biederen Möbelstücken unterschied, in deren Gewand die elektrischen Geräte jener Zeit steckten. Kühn war dagegen Franco Albinis Radioentwurf, der nie in Produktion ging. Ähnliche Ideen wurden erst in den sechziger Jahren wieder aufgegriffen.

Si de nombreux meubles et lampes des années 30 n'ont aucunement vieilli grâce à leurs lignes pures, les appareils de radio et de télévision, qui étaient si modernes à l'époque, paraissent aujourd'hui démodés. C'est le cas du poste de radio en bakélite *Phonola*: par sa ressemblance avec un téléphone, il se distinguait déjà beaucoup des meubles traditionnels camouflant alors les appareils électroniques. En revanche, la radio de Franco Albini était une création audacieuse qui ne fut jamais produite. De telles idées furent reprises dans les années 60.

0024
Upright lamp, crystal and metal
Stehleuchte, Kristallglas und
Metall
Lampadaire, verre de cristal et
métal

Design Giò Ponti, 1931
Fontana Arte
H 190 cm, Ø 55 cm

Luminator
Upright lamp of brass or nickel
Stehleuchte aus Messing oder
Nickel
Lampadaire en laiton ou en nickel

Design Pietro Chiesa, 1933
Fontana Arte
H 190 cm, Ø 22 cm

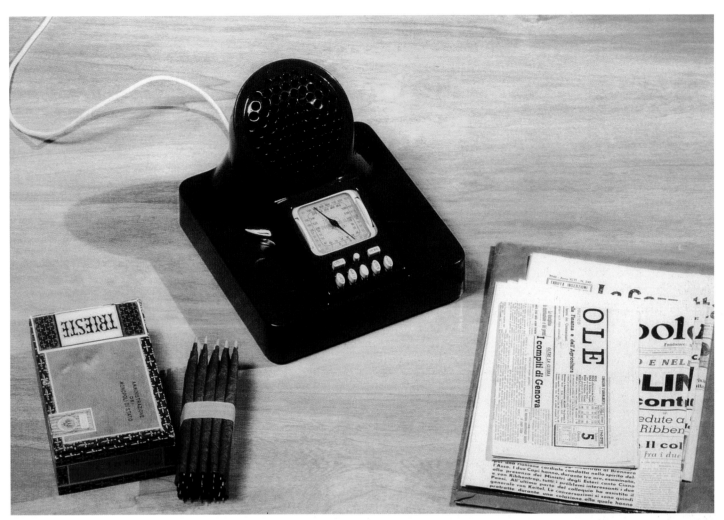

Phonola
Radio with Bakelite casing
Radio mit Gehäuse aus Bakelit
Radio avec boîtier en bakélite

Design Luigi Caccia Dominioni,
Livio and Pier Giacomo
Castiglioni, 1939
Phonola

Television set
Wooden casing
Holzgehäuse
Boîtier en bois

Design and Production Magnetti
Marelli, 1938

Radio
Prototype, acrylic casing,
never manufactured

Prototyp, Gehäuse aus Plexiglas,
wurde nicht produziert

Prototype, boîtier en plexiglas,
n'a pas été produit

Design Franco Albini, 1933

Lingotto Fiat plant

Spiral ramp over which the
finished automobiles were driven
to their test-run on the roof of
the factory.

Spiralenförmige Rampe, über die
fertiggestellte Wagen auf eine
Teststrecke auf dem Dach der
Fabrikanlagen gefahren werden
konnten.

Rampe en spirale sur laquelle on
pouvait tester les voitures et
conduisant au toit de l'usine.

Lancia Coupé Aprilia
Streamlined car, designed by the
Pininfarina workshop in the 1930s

Stromlinienförmiger Wagen, der
in den dreißiger Jahren von der
Karosseriewerkstatt Pininfarina
entworfen wurde

Voiture au profil aérodynamique,
créée dans les années 30 par les
carrossiers Pininfarina

Fiat 500 Topolino
One of the most poular
automobiles of the first half of
this century, manufactured into
the 1950s

Einer der populärsten
Kleinwagen der ersten
Jahrhunderthälfte,
bis in die fünfziger Jahre
produziert

L'une des petites voitures les plus
populaires de la première moitié
du siècle,
fabriquée jusque dans les années
cinquante

Design Dante Giacosa, 1936
Fiat

The automobile's success story began in
the 1930s. The gigantic Fiat plant Lingotto
had already been set up near Turin in the
early 1920s. This was where the *Fiat 500*
and the famous *Topolino* would be produced for the mass market. The streamlined
Lancia Coupé, whose forms were
influenced by American automobiles, was
considered a luxury-class vehicle.

Das Auto trat in den dreißiger Jahren seinen Siegeszug an. Schon zu Beginn der
zwanziger Jahre war bei Turin das giganti-
sche Fiat-Werk Lingotto errichtet worden, in
dem später der *Fiat 500*, der berühmte
Topolino, als Massenauto produziert wurde.
Als Luxusfahrzeug galt das stromlinien-
förmige Lancia-Coupé *Aprilia*, das beein-
flußt ist von den Formen amerikanischer
Automobile.

L'automobile entreprit la conquête du
monde dans les années 30. C'est dans
l'immense usine Fiat Lingotto, construite
près de Turin dans les années 20, que fut
produite en série la *Fiat 500*, le fameux
Topolino. Quant au coupé Lancia *Aprilia* aux
lignes fluides inspirées des automobiles
américaines, il était alors considéré comme
une voiture de luxe.

Between Reality and Utopia

Zwischen Realität und Utopie

Entre la réalité et l'utopie

The Second World War saw the destruction of houses, apartments, industries, furnishings and countless objects necessary to daily life. They all had to be produced again, as quickly as possible.

The post-war years and the 1950s were shaped by the rapid reconstruction of the country, a sense of optimism and a matter-of-fact attitude. Mass production was more in demand than ever before. What was required was lightweight, mobile, versatile furniture and objects that could fit into the generally small apartments that had been put up virtually overnight. Reconstruction and the economic boom also brought prosperity. Italian architects and designers soon had a broad range of tasks. Giò Ponti senior built high-rises and luxury mansions all over the world, furnished bars and casinos, designed cabinets, tables, lamps, cutlery, espresso machines, sanitation objects – and his *Superleggera* chair is still a synonym for the »consummate chair«. It is simple but beautiful, lightweight but sturdy. Carlo Mollino fitted out the homes of his wealthy clients with his swelling, curving furniture. Crafted out of curved wood, his pieces had more in common with sculptures than with traditional furniture.

Marco Zanuso and Osvaldo Borsani have made design history with their eminently sensible designs. Their furniture was meant for the modern, average person and in particular it was furniture that solved problems. Their *D 70* couch was created for a family with a small living-room that wanted to enjoy the view from the window as well as the fireplace on the opposite wall. A clever mechanism allowed the couch to be folded out to two sides or into a bed. Referring to himself and his company, Tecno, Borsani said, »our work is industrial design plus imagination«, while Zanuso sees design as a political responsibility lying between reality and utopia.

Western society became mobile and Italian industry provided an appropriate vehicle for everybody – from the *Vespa* and the *Fiat 500* to the luxurious, convertible sports cars made by Alfa Romeo. A critic would later describe Italy in the 1950s as »unabashedly modern«. But one need only look at the Venini objects to see that »bellezza« – beauty – was still being created.

Häuser, Wohnungen, Industrien, Einrichtungen und Gebrauchsgegenstände waren im Zweiten Weltkrieg zerstört worden und mußten so schnell wie möglich wiederbeschafft werden.

Ein explosionsartiger Wiederaufbau, Optimismus und zugleich Sachlichkeit prägten die Atmosphäre der Nachkriegszeit und der fünfziger Jahre. Stärker als je zuvor war Massenproduktion gefragt, wurden leichte, mobile, vielfältig nutzbare Möbel und Gegenstände benötigt, die in die hastig in Massenbauweise errichteten, meist engen Wohnungen hineinpaßten. Wiederaufbau und Wirtschaftsboom erzeugten auch Wohlstand, und schon bald fand sich für die italienischen Architekten/Designer ein breites Betätigungsfeld. Senior Giò Ponti baute Wolkenkratzer und Luxusvillen in aller Welt, stattete Bars und Casinos aus, entwarf Schränke, Tische, Lampen, Besteck, Espressomaschinen, Sanitärobjekte – und seinen Stuhl *Superleggera*, der noch heute das Synonym für einen »Stuhl an sich« ist, unauffällig und doch schön, leicht und doch stabil. Carlo Mollino stattete reichen Klienten Wohnungen aus mit seinen schwellenden, kurvigen Möbeln aus gebogenen Holzteilen, die Skulpturen verwandter sind als traditionellen Möbeln.

Marco Zanuso und Osvaldo Borsani sind als die Designer der Vernunft in die Geschichte eingegangen. Sie entwarfen Möbel für den modernen Durchschnittsmenschen und vor allem Möbel gegen Probleme. Borsanis Sofa *D 70* wurde geschaffen für eine Familie, die in ihrem schmalen Wohnzimmer – je nachdem – die Aussicht aus dem Fenster oder an der gegenüberliegenden Wand das Feuer im Kamin genießen wollte. Mit einem ausgefeilten Mechanismus läßt das Sofa sich nach zwei Seiten oder zu einer Liege auseinanderklappen. »Unsere Arbeit ist Industrie-Design plus Phantasie«, sagt Borsani über seine Arbeit und die seiner Firma Tecno, während Zanuso Design als politische Aufgabe sieht zwischen Realität und Utopie.

Mobilität erfaßte die westlichen Gesellschaften, und die italienische Industrie schuf die geeigneten Vehikel für jedermann von der *Vespa* über den *Fiat 500* bis zu luxuriös-sportlichen Cabrios von Alfa Romeo. »Hemmungslos modern« sei Italien in den fünfziger Jahren gewesen, schrieb später ein Kritiker. Bei allem wurde jedoch, wie vor allem die Venini-Produkte zeigen, die »bellezza«, die Schönheit, geschaffen.

La Seconde Guerre mondiale ayant détruit les maisons, les appartements, les complexes industriels, les intérieurs et les objets utilitaires, il s'agissait maintenant de tout remplacer au plus vite.

Le climat de l'après-guerre et des années 50 est donc à la reconstruction. L 'optimisme est à l'ordre du jour, mais on garde quand même les pieds sur terre. Les produits fabriqués à la chaîne n'ont jamais été autant en vogue. Il est indispensable de produire des meubles et des objets légers, amovibles et polyvalents qui conviennent à ces appartements généralement étroits, construits à la hâte et en série. La reconstruction et l'essor économique entraînent aussi la prospérité, et un vaste champs d'activités s'ouvre bientôt aux architectes/concepteurs italiens. Le doyen d'âge Giò Ponti construit des gratte-ciel et des villas luxueuses dans le monde entier, il aménage des bars et des casinos, il dessine des armoires, des tables, des lampes, des couverts, des machines à espresso, des articles sanitaires – et sa chaise *Superleggera*. Considérée aujourd'hui encore comme la chaise par excellence, elle est à la fois discrète et belle, légère et solide. Carlo Mollino décore les intérieurs d'une clientèle fortunée avec ses meubles en bois cintré, aux formes amples et arrondies, qui évoquent plus des sculptures que des meubles traditionnels.

Marco Zanuso et Osvaldo Borsani sont entrés dans l'histoire comme concepteurs de la Raison. Leurs meubles s'adressent en effet à l'Italien moyen et ont été créés pour répondre à un problème. C'est ainsi que le canapé *D 70* a été conçu pour une famille qui, dans son petit logement, veut jouir de la vue qu'elle a de sa fenêtre mais aussi de son feu de cheminée à l'autre bout de la pièce. Grâce à son mécanisme ingénieux, on peut rabattre les accoudoirs ou même le dossier, ce qui le convertit en lit. «Design industriel et imagination, voilà ce qui compose notre travail» explique Borsani.

Les sociétés occidentales deviennent mobiles et l'industrie italienne crée des véhicules qui conviennent à tous, de la *Vespa* aux luxurieuses décapotables d'Alfa Romeo, en passant par la *Fiat 500*. En parlant de l'Italie des années 50, un critique devait écrire plus tard qu'elle était «moderne sans retenue». Dans toutes les créations toutefois, c'est la «bellezza», la beauté, qui prime, comme on peut le voir notamment avec les produits Venini.

1945–1959

Living-room of a house furnished by the architect and designer Carlo Mollino 1944 for the art collectors Ada and Cesare Minola in Turin.

Wohnraum eines Hauses, das der Architekt und Designer Carlo Mollino 1944 für das Sammler-ehepaar Ada und Cesare Minola in Turin einrichtete.

Pièce d'une maison aménagée en 1944 par l'architecte et créateur Carlo Mollino pour le couple Ada et Cesare Minola, collectionneurs de Turin.

Workshop of the cabinetmakers Apelli and Varesio in Turin, around 1950. Most of Carlo Mollino's organically shaped furniture was made here.

Werkstatt der Tischlerei Apelli und Varesio in Turin, um 1950. Hier wurde ein großer Teil der Möbel Carlo Mollinos mit ihren organischen Formen hergestellt.

Atelier de la menuiserie Apelli et Varesio de Turin, vers 1950. Une grande partie des meubles aux formes organiques de Carlo Mollino fut fabriquée dans cet atelier.

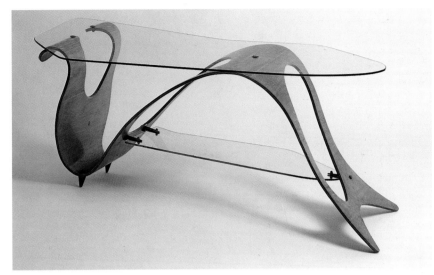

Table of glass and wood with the curved lines typical of the designer

Tisch aus Glas und Holz in der typischen geschwungenen Linienführung des Designers

Table en verre et en bois aux lignes caractéristiques du designer

Carlo Mollino

The Turin architect Carlo Mollino (1905–1973), responsible for organic, often fantastic creations, was one of Italy's most unconventional designers. He designed houses and their furnishings. The swelling forms of much of his furniture have an erotic appeal.

Der Turiner Architekt Carlo Mollino (1905–1973) mit seinen organischen, oft phantastischen Formgebungen war einer der eigenwilligsten Gestalter Italiens. Er entwarf Wohnhäuser und deren Einrichtungen. Die schwellenden Formen vieler seiner Möbel sind von erotischer Anzüglichkeit.

L'architecte turinois Carlo Mollino (1905–1973), grand créateur de formes organiques et souvent fantastiques, fut l'un des designers les plus originaux d'Italie. Il créa des maisons d'habitation ainsi que leur aménagement intérieur. Ses meubles ont par leurs formes tumescentes une connotation érotique.

Chair, designed for Lisa and Giò Ponti
Bronze frame, with two seats and two back rests

Stuhl, entworfen für Lisa und Giò Ponti
Messingrahmen, zweigeteilte Sitzpolster und Rückenlehne

Chaise, conçue pour Lisa et Giò Ponti
Cadre en laiton, assise et dossier en deux parties

Design Carlo Mollino, 1940
Probably Apelli & Varesio

Giò Ponti was one of the most influential architects of the 20th century. He published journals, and designed buildings, interiors and objects of a timeless classicism. His *Superleggera* chair has been described as »the consummate chair«. He worked closely with Piero Fornasetti, whose trompe-l'œil paintings removed Ponti's furniture from the immediate, surrounding reality.

Giò Ponti war einer der einflußreichsten Architekten und Designer des 20. Jahrhunderts. Er gab Zeitschriften heraus, schuf Bauten, Inneneinrichtungen und Objekte von zeitlosem Klassizismus. Sein Stuhl *Superleggera* wurde als »Stuhl an sich« bezeichnet. Er arbeitete eng zusammen mit Piero Fornasetti, der Pontis Möbel mit Trompe-l'œil-Malerei der Realität entrückte.

Giò Ponti est l'un des architectes et designers les plus influents du XXᵉ siècle. Il publia des revues et créa diverses constructions, des intérieurs et des objets d'un classicisme sans âge. Sa chaise *Superleggera* fut qualifiée de «chaise par excellence». Il travailla étroitement avec Piero Fornasetti qui eut l'idée de donner une dimension irréelle à ses meubles par une peinture en trompe-l'œil.

Superleggera
Wooden chair with rush seat,
is still manufactured today

Stuhl aus Holz mit Geflecht aus
spanischem Rohr,
wird heute noch produziert

Chaise en bois, siège paillé,
est fabriquée encore de nos jours

Design Giò Ponti, 1956
Cassina
H 83 cm, B 41 cm, D 47 cm

Giò Ponti

Piero Fornasetti

Cabinet
Designed by Giò Ponti in 1950
and decorated by Piero
Fornasetti in a trompe-l'œil style.
Together, they designed a
number of furniture pieces and
interiors.

Schrank
1950 von Giò Ponti entworfen und
von Piero Fornasetti im Trompe-
l'œil-Stil bearbeitet. Gemeinsam
gestalteten sie eine Reihe von
Möbelstücken und Einrichtungen.

Armoire
Créée en 1950 par Giò Ponti et
Piero Fornasetti dans un style
trompe-l'œil. Ils ont réalisé
ensemble toute une série de
meubles et de décorations
intérieures.

Chair with back rest in the shape
of a Corinthian capital

Stuhl mit Rückenlehne in Form
eines korinthischen Kapitells

Chaise dont le dossier présente
la forme d'un chapiteau
corinthien

Design Piero Fornasetti, 1950

The small apartments of the post-war era required furniture that was flexible, easy to use and versatile. In 1951 the theme of the Ninth Triennale in Milan was »the forms of the useful« and consumer goods and furniture were on display. Production techniques used elsewhere – for example, in the automobile industry – influenced furniture design. The foam rubber used in car seats was also used to pad armchairs and couches. Foam rubber was a new material, brought onto the market by the Pirelli company. A couch had to fold out effortlessly into a bed, as for example Marco Zanuso's sleep-couch or Osvaldo Borsani's famous armchair/couch system *D70/P40*. Its clear form is typical of the 1950s and yet is also timeless.

Flexible, mit wenigen Handgriffen bedienbare und vielseitige Möbel waren in den kleinen Wohnungen der Nachkriegszeit gefragt. Die »Form des Nützlichen« war 1951 das Thema der Neunten Triennale in Mailand, auf der Konsumgüter und Möbel gezeigt wurden. Die Fertigungstechniken anderer Branchen, etwa der Autoindustrie, beeinflußten die Möbelgestaltung. Sessel und Sofas wurden wie Autositze mit Schaumgummi gepolstert, einem neuen Material, das die Firma Pirelli auf den Markt brachte. Ein Sofa mußte sich mühelos zum Bett ausklappen lassen wie Marco Zanusos Schlafcouch oder Osvaldo Borsanis berühmtes Sessel/Sofa-System *D70/P40*. Ihre klare Form ist typisch für die fünfziger Jahre und zugleich zeitlos.

Les logements de l'après-guerre étaient si exigus qu'il fallait des meubles faciles à manier et à usages multiples. La «forme de l'utile» est le thème de la Triennale de Milan en 1951 où sont exposés des biens de consommation et des meubles. Les techniques de fabrication d'autres branches industrielles, telle l'automobile, influèrent beaucoup sur la création de meubles. Fauteuils et canapés étaient rembourrés comme les sièges de voiture avec du caoutchouc-mousse, un tout nouveau matériau que la firme Pirelli venait de lancer sur le marché. Un canapé devait se transformer en lit en un tour de main comme le canapé-lit de Marco Zanuso ou le célèbre système de fauteuil-canapé d'Osvaldo Borsani *D70/P40*. La pureté des formes est typique des années 50 et cependant toujours actuelle.

Sleep-couch
A newly developed mechanism allowed it to be folded out into a bed.

Schlafcouch
konnte mit einem neuen Klappmechanismus in ein Bett verwandelt werden.

Canapé-lit
Pouvait se transformer en lit avec son nouveau mécanisme de pliage.

Design Marco Zanuso, 1955
Arflex

Lady
Armchairs
Polstersessel mit Schaumstoff
Fauteuils rembourré avec de la mousse

Design Marco Zanuso, 1951
Arflex

P 40
Adjustable armchair and couch
system
Sessel- und Sofa-System mit
Verstellmechanismus
Fauteuil et canapé réglables

Design Osvaldo Borsani, 1954
Tecno
H 90 cm, B 72 cm, D 80–150 cm

»The reclining chair is an
extremely simple and elegant
machine for sitting. It has a
retractable foot rest and the
various elements can be adjusted
into 486 positions.«
(Cherie and Kenneth Fehrmann,
1987)

»Der Liegesessel ist eine
Sitzmaschine von größter
Einfachheit und Eleganz; er ist
mit einer einklappbaren
Fußstütze ausgerüstet, und die
diversen Bestandteile können in
486 Positionen gebracht
werden.«
(Cherie und Kenneth Fehrmann,
1987)

«Le fauteuil de relaxation est une
machine pour s'asseoir à la fois
simple et élégante; elle possède
un repose-pieds rétractable et
ses éléments peuvent prendre
jusqu'à 486 positions différentes.»
(Cherie et Kenneth Fehrmann,
1987)

Incalmo
Bottles out of »incalmo«-glass
Flaschen aus »Incalmo«-Glas
Bouteilles en verre «incalmo»

Design Paolo Venini, 1950
Venini
H 31,5/32,5 cm, Ø 8,5/13,5 cm

Chandelier
Coloured Murano glass

Kronleuchter
Farbiges Murano-Glas

Lustre
Verre murano coloré

Design Giò Ponti, 1946
Venini
Ø 60 cm

Morandiane
Bottles of coloured glass
Flaschen aus farbigem Glas
Bouteilles en verre coloré

Design Giò Ponti, Paolo Venini,
1956
Venini
H 44/46 cm, Ø 9 cm

»Glasses like dreams« was how a critic described the products of Venice's Venini glassworks in 1923. The company was formed in 1921 by the Milanese lawyer, Paolo Venini. He wanted to bring new life into the old art of making glass, which had become entrenched in its traditions. From the very beginning Venini – who also designed himself – commissioned artists and architects to design the glass objects.

»Gläser wie Träume« beschrieb 1923 ein Kritiker die Produkte der Glasbläserei Venini in Venedig. Das Unternehmen war 1921 von dem Mailänder Rechtsanwalt Paolo Venini gegründet worden, der die in Traditionen erstarrte alte Glaskunst neu beleben wollte. Von Anfang an zog Venini, der auch selbst entwarf, Künstler und Architekten zur Gestaltung der Glasobjekte heran.

«Des verres comme des rêves», c'est ainsi qu'un critique admiratif décrit en 1923 les produits de la verrerie Venini à Venise. La fabrique avait été fondée en 1921 par Paolo Venini, un avocat milanais qui souhaitait ranimer l'ancien art du verre figé dans les traditions. Dès le début, Venini engagea artistes et architectes à créer des objets en verre.

Vespa
Motor scooter
Motorroller
Scooter

Design Corradino d'Ascanio, 1946
Piaggio
H 88,5 cm, L 167 cm

Italian automobiles and motor scooters stood for an uncomplicated lifestyle. Europe's young people loved Vespas and Lambrettas, drank espressos, and wore Italian clothes and shoes. For many, the Alfa Romeo *Spider* was – and still is – the dream car. But Italy did not only provide dreams. With the production of affordable small cars it also participated in the motorization of the masses.

Italienische Autos und Motorroller verkörperten unkomplizierte Lebensart. Die Jugend Europas liebte Vespas oder Lambrettas, trank Espresso, trug italienische Kleider und Schuhe. Ein *Spider* von Alfa Romeo war – und blieb – das Traumauto vieler. Doch Italien lieferte nicht nur Träume. Mit der Produktion billiger Kleinwagen war es zugleich beteiligt an der Motorisierung der Massen.

Automobiles et scooters italiens symbolisaient un art de vivre décontracté. La jeunesse européenne s'était entichée des vespas et des lambrettas, buvait de l'espresso et achetait des vêtements et des chaussures «Made in Italy». Beaucoup rêvaient d'une «Spider» de la marque Alfa Romeo. Mais l'Italie ne fabriquait pas que du rêve. En produisant des petites voitures pas chères, elle contribuait largement à la motorisation des masses.

Giulietta Spider
Convertible sports car
Sportcabrio
Décapotable de sport

Design Battista Pininfarina, 1954
Alfa Romeo

Fiat 500 Nuova
Small car
Kleinwagen
Petite voiture

Design Dante Giacosa, 1957
Fiat

Isetta
Tiny car
Kleinstwagen
Petite voiture

Firmenentwurf Iso, 1954
Iso, später BMW
H 180,5 cm, B 70 cm

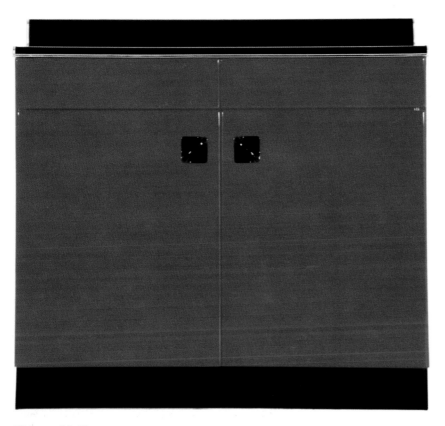

Plastics, new shapes and colours from Italy, enlivened homes and kitchens. Plastics are ideal for mass production, for they are resilient and elastic, lightweight but sturdy. Even the most humdrum objects were designed by architects and thereby acquired an aesthetic quality. The *Mirella* sewing machine by Marco Zanuso was a pioneering design.

Kunststoffe, neue Formen und Farben aus Italien belebten Haushalte und Küchen. Kunststoffe sind ideal für die Massenproduktion, widerstandsfähig und elastisch, leicht und doch stabil. Selbst banalste Objekte wurden von Architekten gestaltet und erhielten so ästhetische Qualität. Die Nähmaschine *Mirella* war ein bahnbrechender Entwurf von Marco Zanuso.

Matières plastiques, formes et couleurs inédites en provenance d'Italie égayaient les intérieurs et les cuisines. Les matières plastiques sont idéales pour la production en série, robustes et élastiques, légères mais stables. Même les objets les plus communs étaient créés par des architectes, ce qui leur donnait une qualité esthétique indéniable. La machine à coudre *Mirella* est une création innovatrice de Marco Zanuso.

Kitchen unit Boffi
Part of a kitchen system

Kücheneinheit Boffi
Teil eines Küchensystems

Elément de cuisine Boffi
Partie d'un ensemble de cuisine

Design Sergio Asti, 1956
Boffi

Mirella
Portable sewing machine
Koffer-Nähmaschine
Machine à coudre portative

Design Marco Zanuso, 1957
Necchi
H 33 cm, B 45 cm, T 17 cm

Compressed to one tenth of their volume
and vacuum-packed, the chairs in the UP
Series – after early designs by Gaetano
Pesce for C & B (Cassina & Busnelli)-
could be effortlessly taken home. With its
opulent curves, the *UP 5 – Donna –* was a
particularly popular, soft refuge, a typical
piece of 1960s Pop furniture. The *Boalum*
lamp also avoided edges and the right
angle and could nestle into every environment. A common feature of many of these
products was their short lifespan, for foam
rubber deteriorates very quickly. Only a few
of these typical pieces from the 1960s have
withstood the test of time, particularly if
they were used regularly.

Auf ein Zehntel ihres Volumens zusammen-
gepreßt, luftdicht und flach in Folie ein-
geschweißt, ließen sich die Sessel der Serie
UP – nach frühen Entwürfen Gaetano
Pesces für C & B (Cassina & Busnelli) –
mühelos nach Hause tragen. *UP 5 – Donna*
– mit ihren üppigen Rundungen war ein
besonders beliebter weicher Zufluchtsort,
ein typisches Popmöbel der sechziger
Jahre. Auch die Lampe *Boalum* meidet das
Kantige, den rechten Winkel und schmiegt
sich jeder Umgebung an. Gemeinsam ist
vielen dieser Produkte, daß sie nicht haltbar
waren, da vor allem Schaumstoff schnell
verfällt. Nur wenige dieser typischen Möbel
der sechziger Jahre haben, besonders wenn
sie viel benutzt wurden, die Zeit überlebt.

Comprimés à un dixième de leur volume,
imperméables à l'air et soudés dans une
feuille de plastique, les sièges de la série
UP – d'après des modèles originaux de
Gaetano Pesce pour C & B (Cassina et
Busnelli) – étaient faciles à transporter. Le
siège *UP5*, baptisé *Donna*, est un meuble
accueillant, très typique des années 60 et
aimé pour ses formes généreuses et son
moelleux. La lampe *Boalum* évite elle aussi
les aspérités, les angles droits et s'adapte à
tous les intérieurs. Le manque de solidité
était une caractéristique commune de ces
meubles, la mousse s'abîmant vite. Seuls
quelques-uns de ces meubles très «années
soixante» ont survécu au temps malgré un
usage répété.

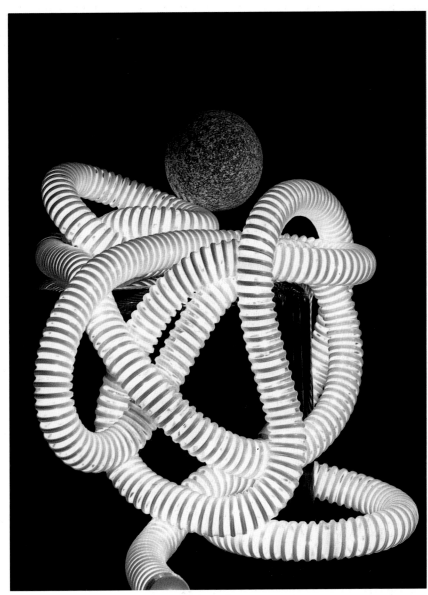

Boalum
Lamp made out of a plastic tube
Lampe aus einem
Kunststoffschlauch
Lampe en tuyau plastique

Design Livio Castiglioni,
Gianfranco Frattini, 1969
Artemide
L 200 cm, Ø 6 cm

Poker
Card table of steel, plastic
laminate and felt
Spieltisch aus Stahl,
Plastiklaminat und Filz
Table de jeu en acier, laminé de
plastique et feutre

Design Joe Colombo, 1968
Zanotta
H 72 cm, B 98 cm, L 98 cm

Joe Colombo

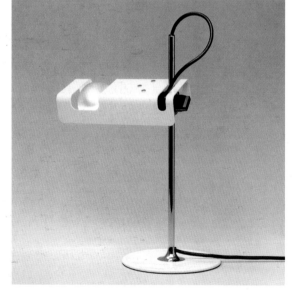

Spider
Metal desk lamp
Schreibtischlampe aus Metall
Lampe de table en métal

Design Joe Colombo, 1966
OLuce
H max. 100 cm

There are few designers who had such a decisive influence on the style of the 1960s as Joe (Cesare) Colombo (1930–1971) He was a visionary and at the same time a very practical designer. The homes which he conceived were far ahead of their time, but always had the inhabitants' needs as their central concern. He designed Utopian environments (p. 75) and useful furniture out of plastic, but was also a virtuoso in his command of such difficult materials as plywood and high-grade steel. His designs are modern and yet at the same time still convey a sense of security.

Joe (Cesare) Colombo (1930–1971) hat wie wenige andere Designer den Stil der sechziger Jahre geprägt. Colombo war ein visionärer und zugleich sehr praktischer Entwerfer. Er konnte sich zukunftsweisende Wohnwelten vorstellen, die jedoch stets die Bedürfnisse des Menschen im Mittelpunkt sahen. Er entwarf utopische Environments (S. 75) und nützliches Mobiliar aus Kunststoff, beherrschte zugleich virtuos den Umgang mit so schwierigen Materialien wie Sperrholz und Edelstahl. Seine Entwürfe sind modern und vermitteln dennoch Geborgenheit.

Le style des années 60 doit beaucoup à Joe (Cesare) Colombo (1930–1971). Colombo était un visionnaire doté d'un grand sens pratique. Il pouvait imaginer des univers habitables futuristes mais sans perdre de vue les besoins humains. Créateur d'environnements utopiques (p. 75), de meubles fonctionnels en matière plastique, il était aussi un virtuose du travail sur des matériaux difficiles, tels le contreplaqué et l'acier spécial. Ses créations sont modernes mais il émane d'elles une impression sécurisante.

Living-room
contains his chair of smooth wood, Model *4801*, 1963, and his *Spider* lamp

Wohnraum
Design Joe Colombo, 1963, mit dem von ihm entworfenen Schichtholzstuhl Modell *4801*, 1963, und seiner Lampe *Spider*

Intérieur
avec sa chaise en bois lamellé de 1963 et sa lampe *Spider*

Blow
Inflatable chair of PVC sheeting
Aufblasbarer Sessel aus PVC-
Folie
Fauteuil gonflable en CPV

Design Carla Scolari, Donato
D'Urbino, Paolo Lomazzi,
Jonathan de Pas, 1967
Zanotta
H 83 cm, B 110 cm, D 110 cm

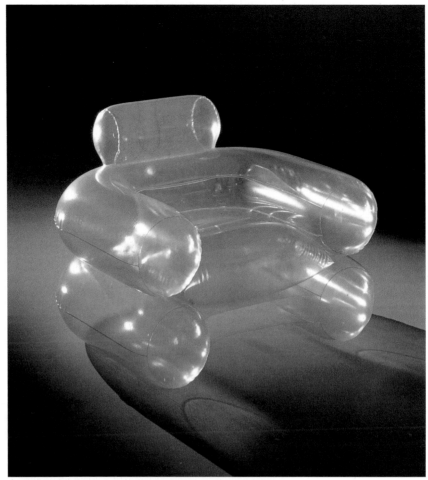

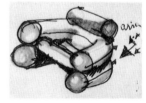

Zanotta stand at the Eurodomus 3, Turin
The *Blow* (shown here with the
designer Paolo Lomazzi) was a
cult object in the 1960s. It could
be found in the apartments of the
young and trendy and beside the
swimming pools of the more
established.

Stand der Firma Zanotta auf der
Eurodomus 3, Turin
Der Sessel *Blow* (hier mit dem
Designer Paolo Lomazzi) war das
Kultmöbel der sechziger Jahre.
Es fehlte weder in den Woh-
nungen schicker junger Leute
noch in den Swimmingpools der
Etablierten.

Stand de la firme Zanotta à
l'Eurodomus 3, Turin
Dans les années 60, un véritable
culte était voué au fauteuil *Blow*
(ici avec le créateur Paolo
Lomazzi). Il avait sa place dans
les appartements des jeunes
BCBG mais aussi au bord des
piscines.

Design De Pas, D'Urbino,
Lomazzi, Scolari, 1967

Blow
Design sketch
Entwurfszeichnung
Etude

Design De Pas, D'Urbino,
Lomazzi, Scolari, 1967

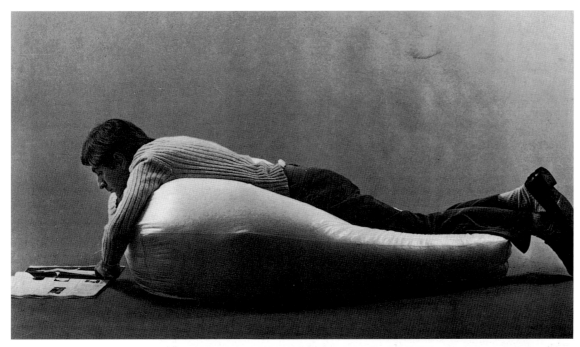

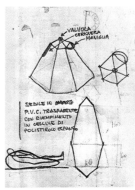

Design sketch for the chair's cover

Entwurfszeichnung für die Hülle des Sessels

Etude pour la housse du fauteuil

Design Gatti, Paolini and Teodoro, 1967/68

Sacco

The polystyrene pellets in the filling can accomodate all possible positions of the human body.
This made *Sacco* into the consummate piece of Pop furniture.

Die Kunststoffkugelfüllung unterstützt alle möglichen Sitz- und Liegepositionen.
Damit wurde *Sacco* zu *dem* Pop-möbel.

N'importe quelle position assise ou couchée est possible sur ce fauteuil rempli de petites billes synthétiques.
Sacco est devenu *le* meuble pop.

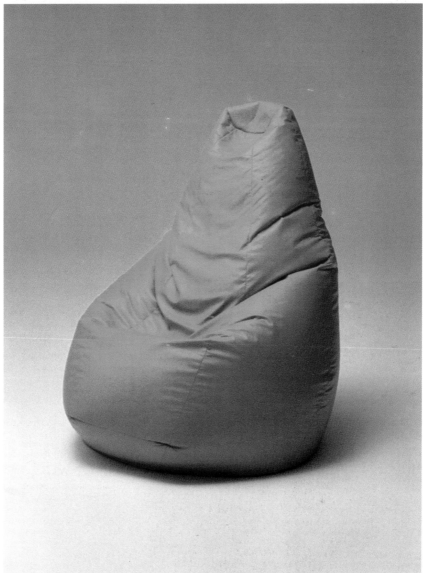

Sacco
Vinyl-covered chair filled with polystyrene pellets
Sessel aus Kunstleder, gefüllt mit Kunststoffkugeln
Fauteuil en cuir rempli de billes synthétiques

Design Piero Gatti, Cesare Paolini, Franco Teodoro, 1968/69
Zanotta
H 68 cm, B 80 cm, D 80 cm

The new technique employed in the mass production of plastic furniture also led to the emergence of a new aesthetics. Designers had to stiffen the material with folds, grooves and bulges, for it was particularly chairs that required a high load-bearing capacity. Moreover, because most of the chairs had to be stackable this also resulted in new design features. Nevertheless, Italian designers successfully skirted the potentially banal and cheap features of this new material and created timeless objects of a high aesthetic quality. The unconventional shapes and colours of the new plastic chairs, their uncomplicated and casual character, reflected the lifestyle of the »swinging Sixties« They still have not lost anything of their modernity.

Die neue Produktionstechnik bei der Massenherstellung von Kunststoffmöbeln ließ auch eine neue Ästhetik entstehen. Mit Falten, Rillen und Wölbungen mußten die Designer das Material versteifen, damit vor allem Stühle belastbar wurden. Zudem sollten die meisten Sitze stapelbar sein, was ebenfalls neue Gestaltungsmerkmale mit sich brachte. Dennoch gelang es den italienischen Designern, dem neuen Material den Beigeschmack des Banalen und Billigen zu nehmen und zeitlose Objekte von hohem ästhetischen Wert zu schaffen. Die unkonventionellen Formen und Farben dieser Kunststoffmöbel, ihre Unkompliziertheit und Beiläufigkeit entsprachen dem Lebensgefühl der »swinging sixties«, und sie haben auch heute nichts von ihrer Modernität verloren.

Les techniques modernes de production en série de meubles en plastique firent naître une esthétique nouvelle. Il fallait pour fabriquer des objets solides, surtout des chaises, que les designers arrivent à solidifier le matériau avec des plis, des moulures et des arrondis. Puis, la plupart des sièges devant être empilables, des innovations s'avérèrent nécessaires aussi dans ce domaine. Les designers réussirent cependant à enlever au plastique son aspect commun et bon marché et à créer des objets esthétiques et intemporels. Le climat des «swinging sixties» se retrouve dans les formes et les coloris originaux de ces meubles en plastique, dans leur côté décontracté et accessoire, qui aujourd'hui encore n'ont rien perdu de leur modernité.

Model 4860
Stacking chair of plastic
Stapelstuhl aus Kunststoff
Chaise empilable en plastique

Design Joe Colombo, 1968
Kartell
H 71 cm, B 42 cm, D 50 cm

Toga
Armchair of plastic
Kunststoffsessel
Fauteuil en plastique

Design Sergio Mazza, 1969
Artemide
H 64 cm, B 80 cm, D 80 cm

Central Living Block
A model habitat presented at the »Visiona«, an exhibition by Bayer AG, held during the International Furniture Fair in Cologne, with Kartell's *4860* stackable chairs.

Wohnmodell, vorgestellt auf der »Visiona«, einer Ausstellung der Bayer AG während der Internationalen Möbelmesse in Köln, mit den Stapelstühlen *4860* von Kartell.

Modèle d'intérieur présenté à la «Visiona», exposition de la Bayer AG tenue pendant le Salon du Meuble à Cologne.

Design Joe Colombo, 1969

Perhaps only an Italian could design a typewriter to be used during one's leisure time. A critic wrote that Ettore Sottsass' *Valentine* was made »to be used everywhere except in the office«. It could accompany poets under blossoming apple trees, be taken along to the football stadium or placed on a bicycle. Rudi Dutschke wrote on one and Olivetti's advertising suggested that Piero di Cosimo would have used one. In general, during this era more attention was paid to the question of a friendlier office environment, as shown by the *Graphis* system. Gino Valle had a huge success with his digital clock *Cifra 3*; a world-wide hit, it was awarded prizes and taken into museum collections.

Eine Schreibmaschine mit hohem Freizeitwert zu schaffen konnte vielleicht nur einem Italiener gelingen. Die *Valentine* von Ettore Sottsass, schrieb ein Kritiker, sei geschaffen, »überall außer im Büro gebraucht zu werden«. Poeten konnten sie unter blühende Apfelbäume tragen, ins Fußballstadion und auf dem Fahrrad ließ sich das handliche Objekt mitnehmen. Rudi Dutschke schrieb darauf, und auch Piero di Cosimo hätte sie benutzt, suggerierte die Werbung des Olivetti-Konzerns. Generell begann das Nachdenken über eine freundlichere Gestaltung der Bürowelt, wie das System *Graphis* zeigt. Ein großer Wurf gelang Gino Valle mit seiner Digitaluhr *Cifra 3*, die einen Siegeszug um die Welt antrat, mit Preisen ausgezeichnet und in Museumssammlungen aufgenommen wurde.

Seul, peut-être, un Italien était capable de créer une machine à écrire réservée aux loisirs. Un critique écrit que la *Valentine* d'Ettore Sottsass a été conçue «pour être utilisée partout sauf au bureau». Il paraît qu'elle accompagnait des poètes sous des pommiers en fleurs, qu'elle se transportait facilement, dans un stade ou sur une bicyclette. Selon la publicité d'Olivetti, Rudi Dutschke l'aurait utilisée, ainsi que Piero di Cosimo. On commençait déjà à réfléchir sur un aménagement plus humain de l'espace travail, comme en témoigne le système *Graphis*. Gino Valle réussit un coup de maître avec son horloge numérique *Cifra 3* qui conquit le monde entier, reçut de nombreux prix et fut achetée par des musées pour leurs collections.

Valentine
Portable typewriter with a red ABS synthetic casing
Reiseschreibmaschine mit Gehäuse aus rotem ABS-Kunststoff
Machine à écrire portative et couvercle rouge en plastique ABS

Design Ettore Sottsass and Perry A. King, 1969
Olivetti
H 11,5 cm, B 34 cm, D 35 cm

Valentine
Plastic model of the typewriter
Kunststoffmodell der Schreibmaschine.
Modèle en plastique de la machine à écrire.

Graphis

Office furniture series with the
Modus 5 chair
Büromöbelserie mit dem Stuhl
Modus 5
Gamme de meubles de bureau
avec la chaise Modus 5

Design Osvaldo Borsani, Eugenio
Gerli, 1968
Tecno

Cifra 3

Digital quartz desk clock
Schreibtischquarzuhr mit
Digitalanzeige
Pendule de bureau à quartz avec
affichage digital

Design Gino Valle, 1965
Solari Udine
H 9,5 cm, Ø ca 10 cm

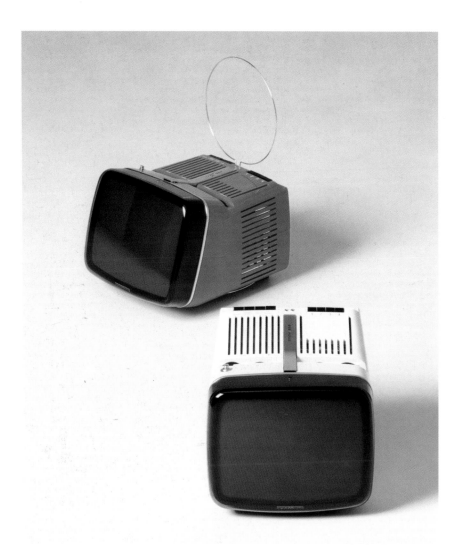

In the early 1960s the Brionvega company commissioned Marco Zanuso and Richard Sapper to develop a new generation of television sets and radios. The designers took the sets – which until then had been designed to resemble conventional furniture – and emphasized their technological and communicative functions. Each of the sets that they designed had its distinctive features. The screen on *Algol 11*, for example, was turned upwards, in Zanuso's words, »like a dog«. The *TS 502* and *Black 201* conceal their function when they are not being used. The radio can be folded together into an anonymous box with a handle, and when it is turned off the television set changes into a mysterious black cube.

Zu Beginn der sechziger Jahre beauftragte die Firma Brionvega Marco Zanuso und Richard Sapper, eine neue Generation von Fernsehapparaten und Radios zu entwickeln. Die Designer nahmen den Geräten den bislang üblichen repräsentativen Möbelcharakter und betonten die technische und kommunikative Funktion. Jedes der von ihnen geschaffenen Geräte hat seine Eigenarten. *Algol 11* zum Beispiel wendet seinen Bildschirm »wie ein Hund« nach oben, wie Zanuso bemerkte. *TS 502* und *Black 201* verbergen ihre Funktion, wenn sie nicht aktiv sind. Das Radio läßt sich zu einem anonymen Kasten mit Henkel zusammenklappen, und der ausgeschaltete Fernseher verwandelt sich in einen rätselhaften schwarzen Würfel.

Au début des années 60, l'entreprise Brionvega chargea Marco Zanuso et Richard Sapper de créer une nouvelle génération de postes de télévision et de radio. Les designers débarrassèrent les appareils de leur caractère traditionnel de meubles imposants en soulignant leur fonction technique et communicatrice. Chacune de leurs créations a ses caractéristiques propres . *Algol 11* oriente par exemple son écran vers le haut «comme un chien», selon l'expression de Zanuso. *TS 502* et *Black 201* dissimulent leur fonction lorsqu'ils ne sont pas en activité. La radio se transforme en un coffre anonyme muni d'une poignée, la télévision en un cube noir énigmatique.

Algol 11
Portable television
Tragbarer Fernseher
Téléviseur portatif

Design Marco Zanuso, Richard Sapper, 1962
Brionvega
H 23 cm, B 27 cm, D 32 cm

TS 502
Fold-away transistor radio
Aufklappbares Transistorradio
Transistor articulé

Design Marco Zanuso, Richard Sapper, 1964
Brionvega
H 13 cm, B 22 cm, D 13 cm

TV Aster 20
Television
Fernseher
Téléviseur

Design Mario and Dario Bellini,
1969
Brionvega
H 73,4 cm, B 47,3 cm, D 39,2 cm

Black 201
Television
Fernseher
Téléviseur

Design Marco Zanuso, Richard
Sapper, 1969
Brionvega
H 34,5 cm, B 40 cm, D 32 cm

Marco Zanuso   **Richard Sapper**

Dino 308 GT
Design Nuccio Bertone, 1970/71
Ferrari

Giulietta GTV
Design Nuccio Bertone, 1966
Alfa Romeo

Montreal
Design Nuccio Bertone, 1967
Alfa Romeo

Automobiles have been the most conspicuous area of Italian design. It made history here, shaping tastes for generations and even playing a role in the breakthrough of the Japanese car into the European market. The old master Nuccio Bertone designed the most beautiful Alfa Romeo Coupés of the post-war era. They included the *Giulietta Sprint* (1954), The *GT Junior* (1966), the *GTV* and the *Montreal*. The latter's name resulted from the fact that it was first presented to the world (as a prototype) at the Montreal Exposition in 1967. The *Dino 308 GT* is one of the more rare Ferrari Coupés designed by Bertone 1971/72.

Augenfälliger als auf jedem anderen Gebiet hat italienisches Design von Automobilen Geschichte gemacht, den Geschmack von Generationen geprägt und, zum Beispiel, japanischen Autos auch in Europa zum Durchbruch verholfen. Altmeister Nuccio Bertone schuf die schönsten Alfa Romeo-Coupés der Nachkriegszeit. Etwa die *Giulietta Sprint* (1954) oder die *GT Junior* (1966), die *GTV* und die *Montreal*, so benannt, weil sie als Prototyp ihre Premiere auf der Weltausstellung 1967 in Montreal feierte. Der *Dino 308 GT* ist eines der selteneren Ferrari-Coupés von Bertone, 1971/72 entworfen.

Plus que dans tout autre domaine, c'est dans celui de l'automobile que le design italien est entré dans l'histoire, a influencé le goût de plusieurs générations et a, par exemple, aidé les voitures japonaises à percer aussi sur le marché européen. Le vieux maître Nuccio Bertone a créé les plus belles Alfa Romeo Coupés de l'après-guerre, comme par exemple la *Giulietta Sprint* (1954), la *GT Junior* (1966), la *GTV* et les *Montréal* qui furent ainsi nommées parce qu'elles furent présentées la première fois comme prototypes à l'exposition mondiale de Montréal en 1967. La *Dino 308 GT* est l'un des rares coupés créés par Bertone pour Ferrari. Il l'a conçue en 1971/72.

Plastics were the big event of the 1960s. As the chemical industry produced an ever greater diversity of materials, the range of objects that could be made from plastic also broadened. The small pieces of furniture made of ABS plastic were particularly popular. These colourful objects, that allowed for many variations, could also be stacked and augmented by further pieces.

Kunststoff blieb das große Thema der sechziger Jahre. Je größer die Vielfalt der Materialien, die die chemische Industrie produzierte, um so breiter wurde die Palette der Objekte, die man aus Kunststoff produzierte. Besonders beliebt waren Kleinmöbel aus ABS-Kunststoff, die sich stapeln, anbauen und variieren ließen, oder farbenfrohe Gebrauchsgegenstände.

Le plastique fut la grande affaire des années 60. Plus la variété des matières plastiques produites par l'industrie chimique augmenta, plus la palette des objets fabriqués dans ces différents matériaux s'enrichit. Les petits meubles en matière plastique ABS qui se superposaient, s'ajoutaient et se modifiaient, ou les objets d'utilisation quotidienne éclatants de couleurs étaient très prisés.

Boby
Trolley made of plastic
Rollwagen aus Kunststoff
Table roulante en plastique

Design Joe Colombo, 1968
Bieffeplast
H 53/74 cm, B 43 cm, D 41 cm

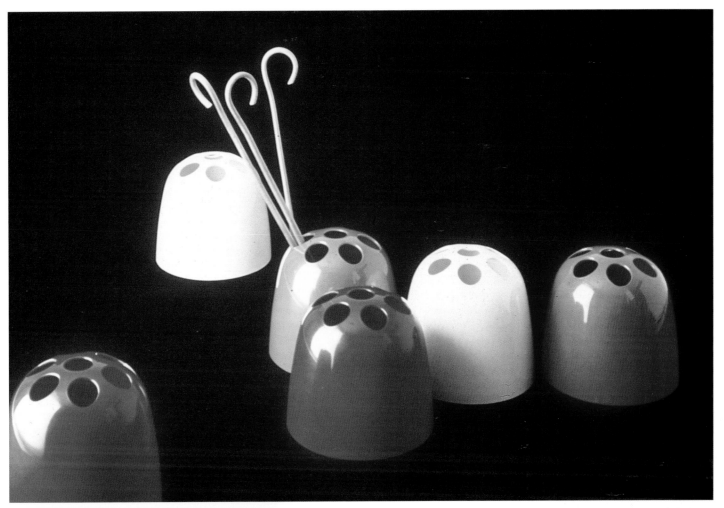

4953
Stacking element made of plastic
Stapelelement aus Kunststoff
Elément empilable en plastique

Design Anna Castelli Ferrieri,
1969
Kartell
Basic element H 23,5 cm,
Ø 42 cm

Dedalo
Umbrella stand of plastic
Schirmständer aus Kunststoff
Porte-parapluies en plastique

Design Emma Schweinberger-
Gismondi, 1966
Artemide
H 40 cm, Ø 38 cm

San Luca
Armchair
Sessel
Fauteuil

Design Achille and Pier Giacomo
Castiglioni, 1961
Gavina
H 96 cm, B 87 cm, D 100 cm

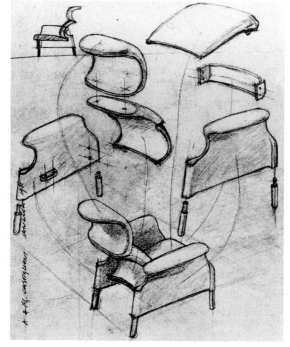

San Luca
Sketch by the Castiglionis for
their armchair assembled of
several parts

Skizze der Castiglionis zu ihrem
aus mehreren Teilen
zusammengesetzten Sessel

Vue éclatée du fauteuil des frères
Castiglioni

Their designs made history. The Castiglioni brothers – Livio (1911–1979), Pier Giacomo (1913–1968) and Achille (1918–) worked together as architects on many projects. The collaboration between Achille and Pier Giacomo after 1945 would prove to be particularly prolific. They created such famous objects as the *Taccia* lamp (p. 29), the *San Luca* armchair, as well as imaginative seating possibilities. Their designs are functional, original and full of ironic undertones. They often used prefabricated pieces such as bicycle seats (p. 27) or tractor seats (p. 85). Whether it be oil and vinegar bottles, chairs or headphones, Achille Castiglioni's designs are distinguished by their apparently effortless, graceful nature.

Ihre Entwürfe haben Design-Geschichte gemacht. Die Brüder Livio (1911–1979), Pier Giacomo (1913–1968) und Achille Castiglioni (geb. 1918) arbeiteten als Architekten gemeinsam an vielen Projekten. Besonders fruchtbar war von 1945 an das Zusammenwirken von Achille und Pier Giacomo Castiglioni, die so berühmte Objekte wie die Lampe *Taccia* (S. 29), den Sessel *San Luca* und phantasievolle Sitzgelegenheiten schufen. Ihre Entwürfe sind funktional, originell und voll ironischer Anspielungen. Oft verwandten sie vorgefertigte Teile wie Fahrradsättel (S. 27) oder Traktorsitze (S. 85). Achille Castiglionis Einfälle haben eine spielerische Anmut, gleich ob er Essig- und Ölfläschchen, Stühle oder Kopfhörer gestaltet.

Leurs créations ont marqué l'histoire du design. Les frères Livio (1911–1979), Pier Giacomo (1913–1968) et Achille Castiglioni (né en 1918), tous trois architectes, ont travaillé ensemble à de nombreux projets. A partir de 1945, la collaboration d'Achille et de Pier Giacomo, en particulier, s'avéra très fructueuse : ils créèrent ensemble des objets célèbres, tels la lampe *Taccia (p. 29),* le fauteuil *San Luca* et des sièges pleins d'imagination. Leurs créations sont originales, fonctionnelles et débordantes d'une ironie sous-jacente. Ils employèrent souvent des objets préfabriqués tels que selles de vélo (p. 27) ou sièges de tracteur (p. 85). Les créations d'Achille, que ce soit un huilier, une chaise ou un casque d'écoute, sont d'un ludisme plein de grâce.

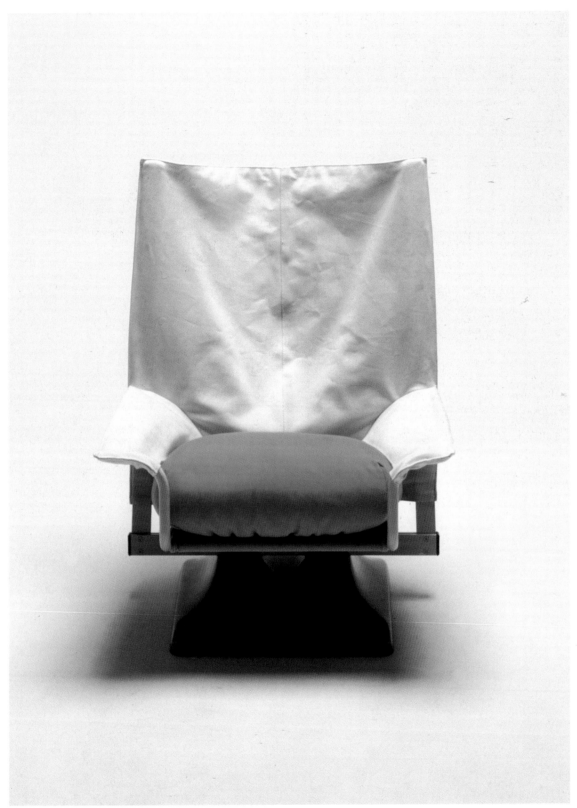

Aeo
Armchair that can be taken apart, plastic and steel with a textile covering
Zerlegbarer Sessel aus Kunst-stoff und Stahl mit Stoffüberzug
Fauteuil démontable en plastique et acier, revêtement en tissu

Design Paolo Deganello/
Archizoom, 1973
Cassina
H 107 cm, B 79 cm, D 70 cm

Alfasud
Design Giorgio Giugiaro, 1971
Alfa Romeo

Alfa Romeo Giulia
Design Giuseppe Scarnati, 1960
Alfa Romeo

Italian lamps are amongst the most successful and well-known products on the international market. Names like *Daphine*, *Tizio* or *Atollo* have achieved international renown not only because they represent new concepts, but also because they are capable of solving every type of lighting problem. The success of *Tizio*, which in 1986 was sold 15 000 times in the United States alone, owes much to its balanced, sculptural character but also to the fact that it is highly functional. At different distances and in different lighting conditions, whether it be a table or an entire room, it can provide the desired amount of light. *Atollo* is valued for the atmospheric quality of its light.

Italienische Lampen gehören zu den erfolgreichsten und bekanntesten Produkten auf dem Weltmarkt. Namen wie *Daphine*, *Tizio* oder *Atollo* sind zu internationalen Begriffen geworden mit ihren neuen Konzeptionen, aber auch mit ihrer Fähigkeit, jede Art von Beleuchtungsproblem zu lösen. Der Erfolg der *Tizio*, die 1986 allein in den USA 15 000mal verkauft wurde, ist sicher einmal auf ihren ausgewogenen Skulptur- und Objektcharakter zurückzuführen, zum anderen auf ihre hohe Funktionalität. In jedem gewünschten Abstand und in unterschiedlicher Helligkeit kann sie Licht auf einer Tischplatte oder in einem Raum dosieren. *Atollo* wird vor allem wegen ihres stimmungsvollen Lichts geschätzt.

Les lampes italiennes comptent parmi les objets les plus célèbres et les plus recherchés sur le marché mondial. Des noms tels que *Daphine*, *Tizio* et *Atollo* sont devenus des références internationales grâce à leur esthétique nouvelle et leur aptitude technique à régler tous les problèmes d'éclairage. Le succès de *Tizio*, qui fut vendue en 15 000 exemplaires aux Etats-Unis pour la seule année 1986, est dû, d'une part, à son aspect équilibré à la fois d'objet et de sculpture et, d'autre part, à son caractère fonctionnel très élaboré. Elle peut moduler la lumière sur un dessus de table ou dans une pièce à la distance et à l'intensité voulues. *Atollo* est surtout appréciée pour sa lumière d'ambiance.

Atollo
Table lamp, painted aluminium
Tischlampe aus lackiertem
Aluminium
Lampe de table en aluminium
laqué

Design Vico Magistretti, 1977
OLuce
H 70 cm, Ø 50 cm

Interior designed in 1970s.
In the background is a marble
table from the Cenacolo series.

Interieur aus den siebziger
Jahren.
Im Hintergrund links ein Tisch der
Serie Cenacolo aus Marmor.

Intérieur
des années 70.
Au fond à gauche, une table en
marbre de la série Cenacolo.

Design Giulio Cappellini, 1975
Cappellini

Servomuto
Side table, plastic and steel
Beistelltisch aus Kunststoff und
Stahl
Table basse en plastique et acier

Design Achille Castiglioni, 1974
Zanotta
H 86 cm, Ø 50 cm

Cumano
Folding table of painted steel
Klapptisch aus lackiertem Stahl
Table pliante en acier laqué

Design Achille Castiglioni, 1979
Zanotta
H 70 cm, Ø 55 cm

Like familiar acquaintances, one encounters Italian tables – whether small and casual or large and impressive – in apartments, hotels and offices all over the world. Made of plastics, painted metal, marble, granite, travertine, wood or plastic laminates, they have often been poured, glued or polished and can usually be had in many different sizes. Common to all of them is their clear, matter-of-fact character, and unpretentious elegance. Two popular tables are *Servo-muto*, a dumb waiter that can be easily moved, and the practical *Cumano*, that can be folded up and hung on the wall. The marble table *Cenacolo* is more imposing and can be used both for dining and as a desk.

Wie guten Bekannten begegnet man den italienischen Tischen – ob klein und beiläufig oder stabil und repräsentativ – auf der ganzen Erde in Wohnungen, Hotels, Büros. Sie sind aus Kunststoff, lackiertem Blech, aus Marmor, Granit, Travertin, Holz oder Kunststofflaminaten gefertigt, gegossen, geleimt, geschliffen und meist in vielen Größen zu haben. Allen gemeinsam sind die Klarheit und Selbstverständlichkeit, die unprätentiöse Eleganz. Zwei weitverbreitete und beliebte Helfer sind der *Servomuto*, der stumme Diener, der sich leicht an seinem Knopf transportieren läßt, und der praktische *Cumano*, der sich klappen und an die Wand hängen läßt. Repräsentativ wirkt der Marmortisch *Cenacolo*, sowohl als Eß- wie als Schreibtisch zu nutzen.

Les tables italiennes sont comme de bonnes connaissances, elles se rencontrent partout dans le monde, dans les appartements, les hôtels, les bureaux, qu'elles soient petites et modestes ou massives et imposantes. Ces tables sont fabriquées, coulées, collées, polies dans presque toutes les tailles et tous les matériaux : en plastique, en métal laqué, en marbre, en granit, en travertin, en bois ou en matière plastique laminée. Elles ont en commun la pureté des lignes, le naturel ainsi que l'élégance modeste et sobre des formes. Très répandus et appréciés pour leur qualités pratiques, il y a *Servomuto*, le valet, qui se transporte facilement grâce à son bouton, et *Cumano*, si pratique, qui se plie et s'accroche au mur. *Cenacolo*, tout de marbre, s'utilisant aussi bien comme table- repas que comme bureau, est un meuble qui en impose.

Instrumenta
Cutlery out of high-grade steel
Besteck aus Edelstahl
Couverts en acier inoxydable

Design Lino Sabattini, 1978
Sabattini Argenteria

The rising standard of living in the western world, its pursuit and refinement of the pleasures of life, also led to an interest in attractive household appliances. Italian kitchen appliances became as popular as its cuisine. *La Pavoni* had a technological and functional appeal but, as a small steam engine, also had a nostalgic charm. One of the most popular espresso machines, it is also a status symbol.

Mit dem steigenden Wohlstand der westlichen Gesellschaften, ihrer Hinwendung zum Genuß und dessen Verfeinerung, wuchs das Interesse an schönem Haushaltsgerät. Wie die Kochkunst Italiens wurde sein Küchengerät begehrt. *La Pavoni* mit der technisch-funktionalen und zugleich nostalgischen Ausstrahlung einer kleinen Dampfmaschine ist eine der beliebtesten Espressomaschinen und Statussymbol.

Avec la prospérité grandissante des sociétés occidentales, leurs tendances hédonistes et la recherche du raffinement, se développa aussi l'intérêt pour les beaux ustensiles ménagers. Ceux que l'Italie se mit à fabriquer devinrent aussi célèbres que sa cuisine. *La Pavoni*, une cafetière à pression alliant technique fonctionnelle et charme nostalgique, est une des préférées parmi les machines à espresso, symboles de standing.

La Pavoni
Espresso machine, copper and bronze body
Espressomaschine mit Gehäuse aus Kupfer und Messing
Machine à espresso au couvercle en cuivre et laiton

Design Pavoni, 1974–76
Pavoni

Pala
Serving cutlery of silver
Vorlegebesteck aus Silber
Grands couverts en argent

Design Lino Sabattini, 1973
Argenteria Sabattini

Proust

Armchair from the Bauhaus
Collection
Polstersessel aus der Kollektion
Bauhaus
Fauteuil capitonné de la
collection Bauhaus

Design Alessandro Mendini, 1979
Studio Alchimia
H 115 cm, B 105 cm, D 80 cm

Il Mobile Infinito

Furniture system of wood, metal
and plastic. It is comprised of 14
elements that can be put
together arbitrarily. Created by
nearly thirty designers and artists
in 1981.

Möbelsystem aus 14 von rund
dreißig Designern und Künstlern
1981 gestalteten Elementen, die
beliebig kombiniert werden
konnten, aus Holz, Metall und
Kunststoff.

Ensemble aux modulations
variables constitué de 14
éléments qui furent créés en 1981
par une trentaine de designers et
d'artistes. Les éléments en bois,
en métal et en plastique se
modulent entre eux au gré des
inspirations.

H 360 cm, B 82 cm
D 82 cm

Alessandro Mendini doubted that it was still
possible to create a modern design. His re-
designs were ironic reflections of the great
classics of design history and through the
use of pennants and other ornamentation
he placed these in the dimension of kitsch.
By making his *Mobile infinito* changeable,
he has denied it a final form.

Alessandro Mendini zweifelte daran, daß es
möglich sei, noch einen modernen Entwurf
zu machen. Mit seinem Re-Design reflek-
tierte er ironisch die großen Klassiker der
Design-Geschichte. Mit Fähnchen und
anderem Zierat versetzte er sie in die
Dimension des Kitsches. Seinem *Mobile
infinito* versagte er die endgültige Form,
indem er es veränderbar machte.

Alessandro Mendini doutait qu'il fût encore
possible d'innover en matière de création.
Aussi, avec son re-design empreint d'ironie,
réinvente-t-il les grands classiques de
l'histoire du design. Il leur donne une
dimension kitsch par des fanions et autres
décorations et prive son *Mobile infinito* de
sa forme définitive en le rendant modulable.

Alessandro Mendini

Re-Design Thonet
Revised version of the Thonet
Chair 214, 1859
Überarbeitung des Thonet-
Stuhles 214 von 1859
Modification de la chaise Thonet
214 de 1859

Design Alessandro Mendini, 1979
Studio Alchimia
H 90 cm, Ø 41 cm

Vassilij di Breuer
Re-design of the armchair that
Marcel Breuer designed in 1925
for Wassily Kandinsky.

Re-Design des Sessels, den
Marcel Breuer 1925 für Wassily
Kandinsky entwarf.

Nouvelle conception du fauteuil
créé en 1925 par Marcel Breuer
pour Vassili Kandinsky.

Design Alessandro Mendini, 1973
Studio Alchimia
H 85 cm, B 86,5 cm D 63 cm

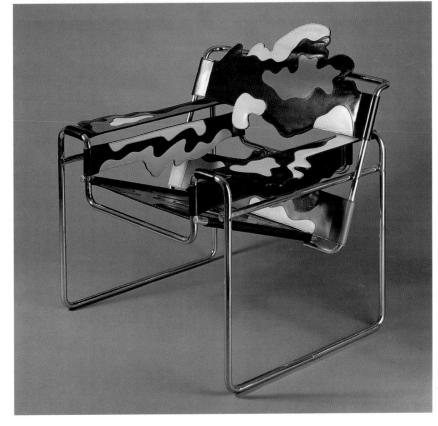

Radicalism and Yearnings

Radikalität und Sehnsucht

Radicalisme et aspirations

The first exhibition on the part of the Memphis Group in September 1981 for an avant-garde public was greeted with almost hysterical enthusiasm. Many people were delighted by the cheerful, optimistic, crazy objects in bright colours, covered with plastic laminates or decorated with colourful light bulbs. After the quiet simplicity and exquisite grandeur in the expensive furniture stores, this was something new. The Zeitgeist, which called for the conspicuous and the garish, was reflected in this furniture and these objects. These were furnishings that would please children and the child in every adult. Functionalism, international Modernism were gone – temporarily(?) – from design. What counted was the object.

Many design critics understood and still understand Memphis as a joke, a provocation, for one could barely sit on the chairs and the shelves provided almost no storage room. But Memphis brought some fresh air into the furniture business and was quickly copied all over the world.

Ettore Sottsass, the initiator of Memphis, soon left the movement behind him, as he has left so much behind him, in order to follow new paths. »I like copies, since they destroy me and somehow revive me. I am separating from Memphis because I have been schematized; I have been eaten up by the copies.« Memphis was certainly the most spectacular, but it was not the only new design movement of the 1980s. The classic Italian line still existed alongside the »bad taste« of which Memphis was often accused. Designs were still created that met the demands for elegant, prestigious furniture and objects. High-Tech furniture, made out of industrial materials, emphasized Functionalist principles. With their sparse aluminium or steel outlines, and their rubber-nubbed seats or rubber back rests, these pieces of High-Tech furniture also have the character of objects. They are meant for the minimalists amongst the design buffs and in their way are as radically modern as Memphis. A further line of design was also developed in the 1980s and found expression above all in the work of Aldo Rossi and Gaetano Pesce. It is distinguished by a concentration on what is essential. It looks back at old traditional forms of furnishings.

Eine nahezu hysterische Begeisterung entfachte die erste Ausstellung der Memphis-Gruppe im September 1981 bei einem Avantgarde-Publikum. Diese fröhlichen, optimistischen, verrückten Objekte in bunten Farben, mit Plastiklaminaten beschichtet oder mit bunten Glühbirnen bestückt, entzückten viele Menschen. Hier war etwas Neues nach all der stillen Einfalt und edlen Größe in den teuren Möbelgeschäften. Der Zeitgeist, der Schrilles, Grelles brauchte, fand sich wieder in den Möbeln und Objekten. Das waren Einrichtungsstücke, die auch Kinder erfreuten – und das Kind in jedem Erwachsenen. Der Funktionalismus, die Internationale Moderne wurden – vorübergehend (?) – aus dem Design verabschiedet. Was zählte, war das Objekt.

Memphis wurde und wird noch heute von vielen Designkritikern als Witz verstanden, als Provokation, da die Stühle kaum zum Sitzen geeignet sind und die Regale kaum Stauraum bieten. Doch Memphis fegte frischen Wind in die Möbelbranche und wurde schon bald auf der ganzen Welt kopiert.

Ettore Sottsass, der Memphis-Initiator, ließ die Bewegung bald hinter sich, wie er schon vieles andere hinter sich gelassen hatte, um einen neuen Weg einzuschlagen: »Ich mag Kopien, da sie mich zerstören und mich irgendwie wiederbeleben. Ich trennte mich von Memphis, weil ich, schematisiert, von den Kopien gefressen wurde.« Memphis war gewiß die spektakulärste, doch nicht die einzige neue Designbewegung der achtziger Jahre. Neben dem »schlechten Geschmack«, der Memphis oft bescheinigt wurde, hielt sich die klassische italienische Linie, entstanden Möbel und Objekte, die auch den Bedarf an edlem, repräsentativem Mobiliar deckten. Eine Steigerung der funktionalistischen Prinzipien brachten die High-Tech-Möbel aus Industriematerialien. Auch sie haben Objektcharakter mit ihren sparsamen, die Umrisse nur markierenden Linien aus Stahl oder Aluminium, mit ihren Gumminoppensitzen oder Gummirollen als Lehnen. Sie sind für die Minimalisten unter den Designanhängern gedacht und ähnlich radikal modern wie Memphis. Noch eine weitere Designlinie entfaltete sich in den Achtzigern, die in den Arbeiten Aldo Rossis oder Gaetano Pesces zum Ausdruck kommt. Sie zeigt eine Rückbesinnung auf Urbedürfnisse menschlichen Daseins.

La première exposition du groupe Memphis déclencha dans le public d'avant-garde un enthousiasme frisant l'hystérie. La gaîté, l'optimisme et le caractère fantasque de ces objets multicolores habillés de laminé en plastique ou pourvus d'ampoules de couleur ravissaient un grand nombre de personnes. Après la monotonie et la majesté des meubles de luxe, on voyait enfin apparaître quelque chose de nouveau. L'esprit du temps qui voulait du criard et du tapageur se reconnaissait dans ces meubles et ces objets. On avait là des articles d'ameublement qui réjouissaient les enfants aussi bien que les adultes. Le fonctionnalisme, les Modernes internationaux, furent – provisoirement (?) – bannis du design. C'était l'objet qui comptait.

Pour beaucoup de critiques du design, Memphis était – et est encore – une plaisanterie, une provocation, puisqu'on pouvait à peine s'asseoir sur ses chaises et que les étagères ne permettaient presqu'aucun rangement. Pourtant Memphis apporta une bouffée d'air frais à l'industrie du meuble et fut bientôt copié dans le monde entier.

Initiateur de Memphis, Ettore Sottsass quitta le mouvement, comme il avait quitté beaucoup d'autres choses, pour s'engager dans une nouvelle voie: «J'aime les copies. Elle me détruisent et me raniment en quelque sorte. Je me sépare de Memphis parce qu'elles m'engloutissent. Ceci dit en simplifiant la situation.» Tout en étant le mouvement le plus spectaculaire des années 80, Memphis n'était pas le seul à être nouveau. A côté du «mauvais goût» souvent reproché aux objets Memphis, il y avait la ligne italienne classique. On voyait apparaître des meubles et des objets répondant au désir d'élégance et d'ostentation. Les principes fonctionnalistes trouvèrent leur superlatif dans les meubles High-Tech fabriqués avec des matériaux industriels. En aluminium ou en métal, ils avaient eux aussi un côté objet avec leurs lignes restreintes au possible, n'indiquant que les contours, leurs sièges à noppes en caoutchouc ou leurs rouleaux en caoutchouc en guise d'accoudoirs. Ils sont destinés aux minimalistes parmi les adeptes du design et leur modernité radicale rappelle celle de Memphis. Les années 80 virent aussi la naissance d'une autre ligne que l'on retrouve dans les travaux d'Aldo Rossi ou de Gaetano Pesce. Elle indique un retour à l'essentiel, aux formes traditionnelles du mobilier.

1980–1989

Aldo Cibic, Andrea Branzi, Michele de
Lucchi, Marco Zanini, Nathalie du Pasquier,
George J. Sowden, Martine Bedin, Matteo
Thun and Ettore Sottsass (from the left)
designed the first collection for the
Memphis movement. It achieved overnight
fame in September 1981 with its exhibition
of crazy, colourful furniture and objects in
Milan's Gallery Arc '74.

Aldo Cibic, Andrea Branzi, Michele de
Lucchi, Marco Zanini, Nathalie du Pasquier,
George J. Sowden, Martine Bedin, Matteo
Thun und Ettore Sottsass (oben v. l.) ent-
warfen die erste Kollektion der Memphis-
Bewegung, die im September 1981 mit einer
Ausstellung ihrer verrückten, bunten Möbel
und ihrer Objekte in der Mailänder Galerie
Arc '74 mit einem Schlag bekannt wurde.

Aldo Cibic, Andrea Branzi, Michele de
Lucchi, Marco Zanini, Nathalie du Pasquier,
George J. Sowden, Martine Bedin, Matteo
Thun et Ettore Sottsass (en haut de gauche
à droite) créèrent la première collection du
mouvement Memphis. Celui-ci connut la
célébrité du jour au lendemain en exposant
ses meubles et ses objets débordants de
couleurs et de folie à la galerie Arc '74 de
Milan en septembre 1981.

Tawaraya
Podium for sitting and reclining,
wood, metal, tatamis
Sitz- und Liegepodium aus Holz,
Metall, Tatamis
Podium, assise et couchage, en
bois, métal, tatamis

Design Masanori Umeda, 1981
Memphis

Super
Lamp, fibreglass and rubber
Standleuchte aus Fiberglas und
Gummi
Luminaire en fibre de verre et
caoutchouc

Design Martine Bedin, 1981
Memphis
H 25 cm, B 50 cm, D 25 cm

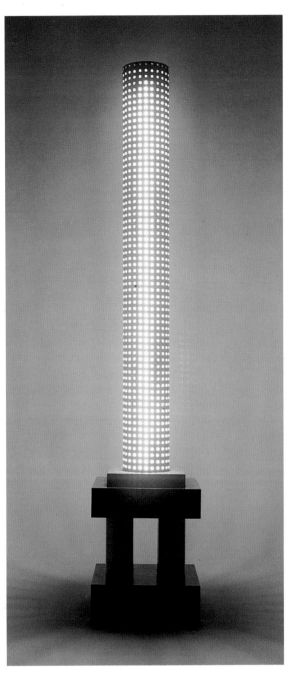

Chicago Tribune
Upright lamp, painted metal
Stehleuchte aus lackiertem
Metall
Lampadaire en métal laqué

Design Matteo Thun, Andrea
Lera, 1985
Bieffeplast
H 190 cm, B 30 cm, D 30 cm

Settimanale
Steel cabinet with seven drawers
Stahlkommode mit sieben
Schubladen
Armoire en acier avec sept tiroirs

Design Matteo Thun, 1985
Bieffeplast
H 160 cm, B 62 cm, D 45 cm

Tavolo con Ruote
Coffee table, glass top on castors
Couchtisch, Glasplatte mit
Laufrollen
Table de salon, plateau en verre
sur roulettes

Design Gae Aulenti, 1980
Fontana Arte
H 25 cm, glass top 120 x 120 cm

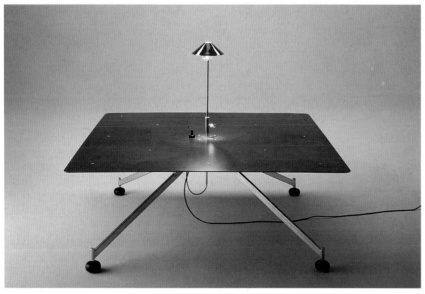

Apocalypse Now
Coffee table of Corten steel with
a lamp
Couchtisch aus Cortenstahl mit
Leuchte
Table de salon en acier Corten
avec luminaire intégré

Design Carlo Forcolini, 1984
Alias
H 45 cm, 90 x 90 / 120 x 120 cm

Although the Memphis spectacle dominated publicity in the 1980s, other design movements were also developing. Independent designers and different ways of life were influential in shaping these developments. Individual firms, such as Alias and its designer Mario Botta, devoted themselves to the continuation of rational design, intensifying it into High-Tech. Gae Aulenti, one of Italy's great architects, created her High-Tech table out of glass and industrial castors in 1980. Carlo Forcolini's *Apocalypse Now* table had a top made out of the same Corten steel that is used for cladding high-rises. It has a severe, technological appearance, as does Paolo Piva's coffee table and Achille Castiglioni's windbreak.

Neben dem Memphis-Spektakel, das publizistisch die achtziger Jahre beherrschte, entwickelten sich andere Designströmungen weiter, geprägt von selbständigen Designerpersönlichkeiten und verschiedenen Lebensformen. Einzelne Firmen wie Alias mit ihrem Designer Mario Botta verschrieben sich der Fortführung des rationalen Designs, das zum High-Tech-Stil gesteigert wurde. Gae Aulenti, eine der großen Architektinnen Italiens, schuf 1980 ihren High-Tech-Tisch aus Glas und Industrie-Laufrollen. Auch Carlo Forcolinis *Apocalypse Now* mit einer Platte aus Cortenstahl, mit dem Hochhäuser verkleidet werden, hat ein technisches Gesicht, ebenso wie Paolo Pivas Couchtisch und Achille Castiglionis Paravent.

A côté de Memphis qui occupa le devant de la scène dans les années 80, d'autres courants se développèrent, marqués par des personnalités indépendantes du design et par des styles de vie différents. Des entreprises, comme Alias et son designer Mario Botta, se consacrèrent au design rationnel qui évolua jusqu'au style high-tech. Gae Aulenti, une des plus grandes architectes italiennes, créa en 1980 sa table high-tech en verre et galets industriels. *Apocalypse Now* de Carlo Forcolini, fait dans un acier Corten dont on revêt les façades de gratte-ciel, a une physionomie technique sévère, tout comme la table basse de Paolo Piva et le paravent d'Achille Castiglioni.

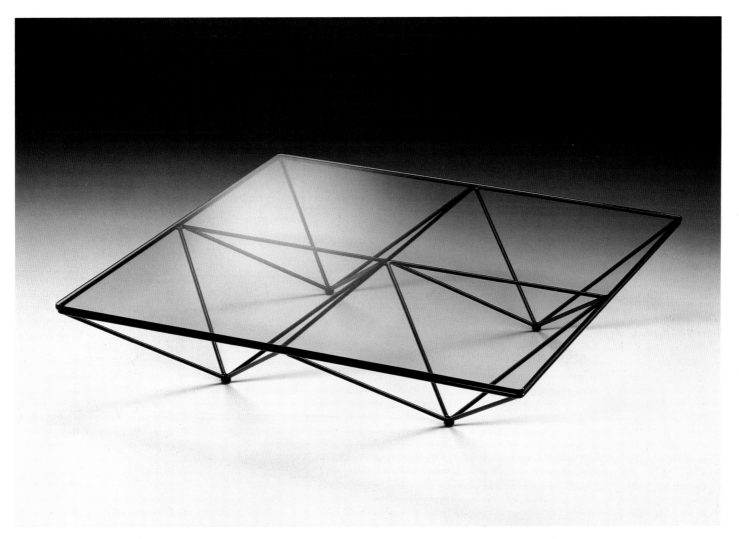

Alanda
Table, glass and steel tubes
Tisch aus Glas und Stahlrohren
Table en verre et tube d'acier

Design Paolo Piva, 1982
B & B
H 25 cm, B 120 cm,
D 60/120/180 cm

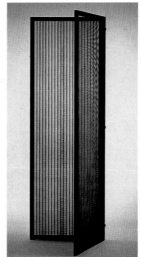

Screen
Windbreak, aluminium and wire
netting
Paravent aus Aluminium und
Maschendraht
Paravent en aluminium et fils
métalliques

Design Achille Castiglioni, 1983
DePadova
H 180 cm, B 120 cm

Spaghetti
Chair, steel frame, back rest of
PVC strips
Stuhl, Stahlrahmen, mit PVC-
Schnur bespannt
Chaise, cadre en bois, cordons
CPV tendus

Design Giandomenico Belotti,
1979
Alias
H 84 cm, B 40 cm, D 51 cm

Tricorno Tre
Clothes rack, steel and plastic
Kleiderständer aus Stahl und
Kunststoff
Porte-manteau en acier et
plastique

Design Enzo Mari, 1980
Danese
H 160 cm, Ø 60 cm

Tangram
Table system comprised of seven
elements
Tischsystem aus sieben
Elementen
Ensemble de sept tables

Design Massimo Morozzi, 1983
Cassina
H 73 cm, table top 170 x 170 cm

4300
Table series out of plastic
Tischserie aus Kunststoff
Série de tables en plastique

Design Anna Castelli Ferrieri,
1982
Kartell
H 72 cm, table top 80 x 80 cm

Mario Botta

Seconda
Chair, metal and polyurethane
Stuhl aus Metall und Polyurethan
Chaise en métal et polyuréthane

Design Mario Botta, 1982
Alias
H 66 cm, B 52 cm, D 58 cm

Tesi, Quinta
Table and chairs of metal
Tisch und Stühle aus Metall
Table et chaises en métal

Design Mario Botta, 1986
Alias
Table: H 74 cm, B 86 cm,
L 240-300 cm

Latonda
Metal chair
Stuhl aus Metall
Chaise en métal

Design Mario Botta, 1987
Alias
H 77 cm, B 63 cm, D 48 cm

Quarta
Chair, aluminium and
polyurethane
Stuhl aus Aluminium und
Polyurethan
Chaise en aluminium et
polyuréthane

Design Mario Botta, 1984
Alias
H 71 cm, B 94 cm, D 65 cm

Samson and Delilah
Table and chairs, poured
polyester
Tisch und Stühle, aus
Polyester gegossen
Table et chaises en
polyester moulé
Design Gaetano Pesce, 1980
Cassina
Table: H 72 cm, L 170–200 cm,
B 150–190 cm
Chair: H 75–89 cm, B 49–71 cm,
D 55–64 cm

Prototype of a mineral water
bottle for Vittel
Prototyp einer Mineralwasser-
flasche für Vittel
Prototype d'une bouteille d'eau
minérale pour Vittel

Design Gaetano Pesce, 1986–89
Vittel

Gaetano Pesce is one of the most unusual designer/artists of the current age. In Italy the borders between art and design were often blurred, and artists and architects sensed an affinity in their thoughts and perceptions. Pesce utterly ignores these borders. He fashions his furniture pieces like sculptures. Daring and sensual, they are linked to a mythical imaginary world, from which he also derives the names for many of his objects. The right angle and the straight line are almost completely absent from Pesce's work. He loves organic forms such as curves, encrusted surfaces, and hollows, which he forms out of plastic. He sees his furniture pieces as parables on the situation in the world at the end of the 20th century.

Gaetano Pesce gehört zu den ungewöhn-lichsten Designerkünstlern der Gegenwart. Häufig waren in Italien die Grenzen zwischen Kunst und Design verwischt, spürten Künstler und Architekten Verwandtschaft im Denken und Empfinden. Pesce ignoriert diese Grenzen vollständig. Er gestaltet seine Möbel wie Skulpturen, kühn, sinnlich und einer mythischen Vorstellungswelt verhaftet, die sich auch in den Namen seiner Objekte widerspiegelt. Der rechte Winkel und die gerade Linie fehlen in Pesces Arbeiten fast völlig. Er liebt orga-nische Formen wie Rundungen, Verkrustun-gen und Höhlen, die er aus Kunststoffen nachformt. Er sieht seine Möbel als Para-beln des Zustands der Welt am Ende des 20. Jahrhunderts.

Gaetano Pesce est l'un des designers les plus originaux de notre époque. En Italie, la frontière était souvent floue entre art et design, les artistes et les architectes étant très proches dans leur manière de penser et de sentir. Pesce ignorait complètement cette limite. Ses meubles sont créés comme des sculptures, hardis, sensuels et attachés à un monde mythique qui se reflète dans les noms qu'il leur donne. L'angle droit et la ligne droite sont presque absents de ses œuvres. Il aime les formes organiques – arrondis, incrustations et creux – qu'il modèle dans des matières plastiques. Il décrit ses meubles comme des paraboles sur l'état du monde en cette fin de siècle.

Tramonto a New York
Couch, plywood, polyurethane
foam
Sofa aus Sperrholz,
Polyurethanschaum
Canapé en contreplaqué, mousse
de polyuréthane

Design Gaetano Pesce, 1980
Cassina
Gesamt: H 120 cm, B 225 cm,
D 105 cm

Sketch
by Gaetano Pesce, some of the
elements of his New York couch

Skizze
Gaetano Pesce mit Elementen
seines New-York-Sofas

Esquisse
de Gaetano Pesce avec les
éléments de son canapé New
York

Photo montage with Gaetano
Pesce and his eight-part couch
»Sunset in New York«

Fotomontage mit Gaetano Pesce
und seinem achtteiligen Sofa
»Sonnenuntergang in New York«

Photomontage avec Gaetano
Pesce et son canapé de huit
éléments «Coucher de soleil à
New York»

Torso
Couch with metal frame,
upholstered
Sofa mit Metallgestell, gepolstert
Canapé avec une structure en
métal, rembourré

Design Paolo Deganello, 1982
Cassina
H 116 cm, B 109–173 cm, D 90 cm

Couches and armchairs have their own characters and reveal a lot about their owners. A person will buy the couch that seems to most reflect his own personality – whether it be severe and discrete, avant-garde, flexible, introverted, or imposing. While Paolo Deganello's *Torso* is related in an elegant and cultivated way to the Memphis style, Gaetano Pesce's chairs display features typical of this designer. *Cannaregio* is a swelling hilly landscape made up of ten differently shaped pieces, none of them similar. His *Feltri* armchairs are made of coloured, stiffened felt and their arm rests can open like the leaves of flowers or close protectively around the occupant.

Sofas und Sessel sind Persönlichkeiten und sagen viel aus über ihre Eigentümer. Ein Mensch wird das Sofa erwerben, dessen Ausdruck seinem eigenen Wesen am meisten entspricht – sei es streng und diskret, avantgardistisch, flexibel, introvertiert oder pompös. Während *Torso* von Paolo Deganello dem Memphis-Stil verwandt ist, dabei jedoch kultiviert und elegant, zeigen die Sitze von Gaetano Pesce typische Merkmale dieses Designers. *Cannaregio* ist eine schwellende Hügellandschaft aus zehn verschieden geformten Teilen, von denen keines dem anderen gleicht. Aus farbigem, versteiftem Filz sind seine *Feltri*-Sessel, deren Lehnen sich wie Blütenblätter öffnen oder sich schützend um den Insassen schließen können.

Les canapés et les fauteuils ont leur caractère propre qui en dit long sur leurs propriétaires. On acquiert généralement le canapé dont l'expression correspond le plus à sa propre personnalité, qu'il soit sévère et discret, avant-gardiste, modulable, introverti ou pompeux. Si *Torso* de Paolo Deganello est apparenté au style Memphis tout en étant cultivé et élégant, les sièges de Gaetano Pesce ont les caractères distinctifs de ce designer. *Cannaregio* est un paysage vallonné tumescent, fait de dix pièces de formes différentes dont aucune ne ressemble à l'autre. Ses fauteuils *Feltri* sont en feutre renforcé coloré, les accoudoirs peuvent s'ouvrir comme des pétales ou se refermer, protecteurs, sur leurs occupants.

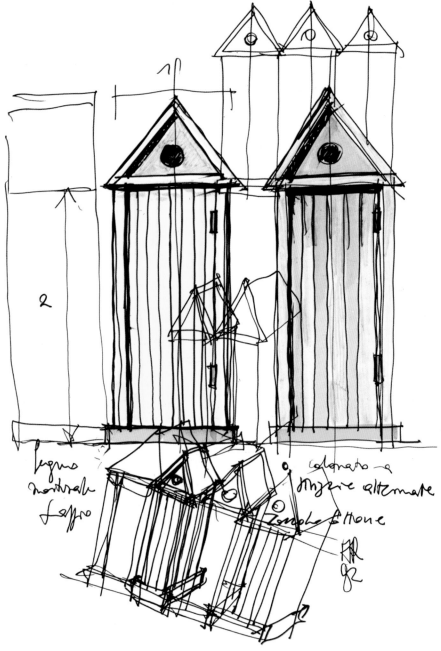

Italian designers have reflected on the basis for their work ever since the debate on their social obligations. In the 1980s a few turned back to the earlier forms of human dwellings and furnishings. Aldo Rossi's wardrobe series *Cabina dell'Elba* recalls historic sentry boxes or old changing cubicles. Rossi has used a variation on a motif that runs through all of his work – from the building to the coffee pot – whose symbolism has to do with the recollection of a happier, more secure time. The same can be said of Antonia Astoris' wardrobe system *Aforismi*, which has strong recollective and emotional qualities.

Gedanken über den Urgrund ihrer Arbeit bewegen italienische Designer seit der Auseinandersetzung um ihren gesellschaftlichen Auftrag. In den achtziger Jahren wandten sich einige zurück zu historischen Formen menschlicher Behausungen und deren Mobiliar. Aldo Rossis Schrankserie *Cabina dell'Elba* erinnert an alte Schilderhäuschen oder Badekabinen. Rossi variiert hier ein Motiv, das sein gesamtes Werk – von der Großarchitektur bis zur Kaffeekanne – durchzieht und dessen Symbolik eine Erinnerung an eine vergangene Zeit, an Heiterkeit und Geborgenheit erkennen läßt. Ähnliches gilt für Antonia Astoris Schranksystem *Aforismi*, aus dem sich Möbel mit starken Erinnerungs- und Gefühlswerten komponieren lassen.

Depuis la discussion sur leur mission sociale, les designers italiens réfléchissent sur la raison d'être de leur travail. Dans les années 80, certains se tournèrent à nouveau vers de vieilles formes d'habitats et de mobiliers. La ligne *Cabina dell'Elba*, une série d'armoires créée par Aldo Rossi, rappelle les anciennes guérites ou les vieilles cabines de bain. Rossi a varié ici un motif qui traverse toute son œuvre – de l'architecture à la cafetière – et dont la symbolique exprime la nostalgie du temps passé, de la sérénité et du sentiment de sécurité. On retrouve le même schéma dans le système d'Antonia Astori *Aforismi* dont les meubles à composer sont porteurs de souvenirs et de sentiments forts.

Cabina dell'Elba
Sketches by Aldo Rossi for his cabinet, available in three sizes and colour combinations

Skizzen Aldo Rossis zu seinen Schränken, die in drei verschiedenen Größen und drei Farbkombinationen lieferbar sind

Esquisses d'Aldo Rossi. Ses armoires existent en trois dimensions différentes et en trois combinaisons de coloris

Medusa
Upright lamp, glass with a steel
base
Stehlampe aus Glas mit Stahlfuß
Lampadaire en verre, socle en
acier

Design Sergio Asti, 1989
Salviati
H 205 cm, Ø 80 cm

In the 1980s the kitchen was transformed into the prestigious centre of domestic life, where amateur cooks could feel that they were professional chefs. High-quality materials such as steel, silver, and precious woods were used in ever more elegant and ingenious ways. Oil and vinegar bottles, even cheese graters, took on an aura of the luxurious.

Die achtziger Jahre machen die Küche zum repräsentativen Mittelpunkt des häuslichen Lebens, in dem Hobbyköche wie Profis wirken können. Edles Material wie Stahl, Silber und wertvolle Hölzer wird in immer eleganteren, ausgefeilteren Formen verarbeitet. Öl- und Essigkännchen, selbst Käsereiben erhalten die Aura des Luxuriösen.

Au cours des années 80, la cuisine est devenue le cœur de la vie familiale, l'endroit privilégié où peuvent opérer professionnels et cordons-bleus. Les matériaux nobles comme l'acier, l'argent et les bois précieux sont travaillés dans des formes de plus en plus élégantes et raffinées. Un halo de luxe entoure jusqu'aux huiliers et râpes à fromage.

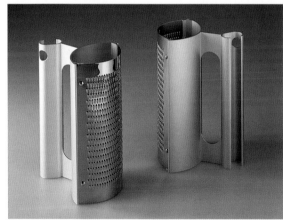

Krios
Modular kitchen system
Modulares Küchensystem
Cuisine à modulation variable

Design Giovanni Offredi, 1983
Abaco/Snaidero

Cheese grater
High-grade steel with an aluminium handle

Käsereibe
Edelstahl mit Aluminiumgriff

Râpe à fromage
Acier inoxydable, manche en aluminium

Design Enzo Mari, 1987
Zani & Zani

Opasis
Table series of high-grade steel
Tischserie aus Edelstahl
Ustensiles de table en acier
inoxydable

Design Enzo Mari, 1986
Zani & Zani
H 4,3–13 cm, Ø 6,2–25 cm

Coffee and tea service
Silver

Kaffee- und Teeservice
Silber

Service à thé et à café
Argent

Design Marco Zanuso, 1981
Cleto Munari

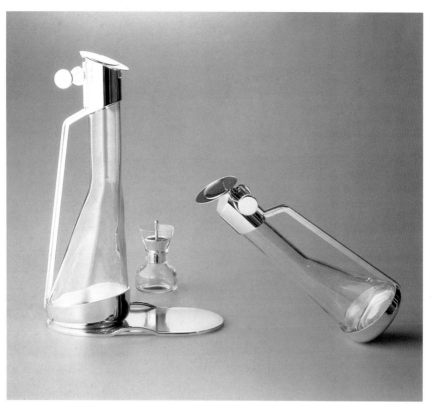

90004/A, 90004/0
Oil and vinegar bottles, glass and
high-grade steel
Essig- und Ölflasche aus Glas
und Edelstahl
Flacons d'huile et de vinaigre en
verre et acier inoxydable

Design Achille Castiglioni, 1984
Alessi
H 18,5/23,5 cm, Ø 6 und 7,5 cm

Cooking has even become the hobby of
high-powered managers and career women.
They want to use good, professional tools.
The Alessi company, which began to produce coffee pots and trays for hotels in
1921, established the branch company
Officina Alessi in 1983. It provided designers
with a chance to seek new forms and refine
existing ones. Richard Sapper worked
together with well-known chefs from Italy
and France to develop *La Cintura di Orione*,
a series of pots and utensils. The shapes
were inspired by old culinary traditions that
reach back into the 16th century.

Kochen ist zum Hobby selbst stark bean-
spruchter Manager und Karrierefrauen geworden, die professionelles, gutes Hand-
werkszeug suchen. Die Firma Alessi, die ab
1921 Kaffeekannen und Tabletts für den
Hotelbedarf produzierte, gründete 1983 den
Firmenzweig Officina Alessi, in dem
Designer neue Formen suchen und über-
lieferte verfeinern. So entwickelte Richard
Sapper mit sechs bekannten Küchenchefs
aus Italien und Frankreich seine Serie *La
Cintura di Orione* mit Töpfen und Utensilien.
Die Formen sind inspiriert von alten
Küchentraditionen, die bis ins 16. Jahr-
hundert zurückreichen.

Cuisiner est devenu le passe-temps des
managers surmenés ou des femmes
carriéristes qui cherchent des outils de professionnels. L'entreprise Alessi, qui a produit à partir de 1921 des cafetières et des
plateaux pour l'industrie hôtelière, fonde en
1983 une filiale, Officina Alessi, où des
designers cherchent des nouvelles formes
et améliorent les anciennes. C'est ainsi que
Richard Sapper et six cuisiniers réputés
d'Italie et de France créent la série *La
Cintura di Orione* composée de casseroles
et d'ustensiles. Les formes sont inspirées
de vieilles traditions culinaires remontant au
XVIᵉ siècle.

La Cintura di Orione
Series of pots and cooking
utensils in high-grade steel,
copper and enamelled cast-iron
Serie von Töpfen und
Kochutensilien in Edelstahl,
Kupfer und emailliertem Gußeisen
Batterie de casseroles et autres
ustensiles de cuisine en acier
inoxydable, cuivre et fonte
émaillée

Design Richard Sapper, 1986
Alessi

9094
Cafetière, high-grade steel and glass
Pressofilter aus Edelstahl und Glas
Percolateur en acier inoxydable et verre

Design Aldo Rossi, 1986
Alessi
H 22/17 cm, Ø 9,8/7,2 cm

9091
Kettle with bronze spout
Wasserkessel mit Flöte aus
Messing
Bouilloire, bec siffleur en laiton

Design Richard Sapper, 1983
Alessi
H 24/19 cm, Ø 20/16,5 cm

Patty Difusa
Wooden chair
Holzstuhl
Chaise en bois

Design William Sawaya
Sawaya & Moroni

Santa
Metal chair with velvet upholstery
Stuhl aus Metall mit
Samtpolsterung
Chaise en métal capitonnée de
velours

Design Luigi Serafini, 1992
Sawaya & Moroni
H 97 cm, B 46 cm, D 40 cm

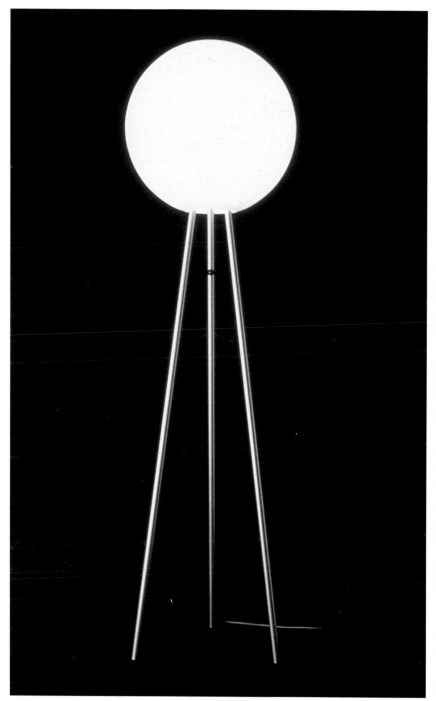

Orbital Terra
Upright lamp, metal and coloured glass
Stehleuchte aus Metall und farbigem Glas
Lampadaire en métal et verre teinté

Design Ferruccio Laviani, 1992
Foscarini
H 170 cm, Ø 53 cm

Prima Signora
Upright lamp, glass and metal
Stehleuchte aus Glas und Metall
Lampadaire en verre et métal

Design Daniela Puppa, 1992
Fontana Arte
H 170 cm, Ø 50 cm

Brera
Upright lamp, metal, glass, plastic
Stehleuchte aus Metall, Glas, Kunststoff
Lampadaire en métal, verre, plastique

Design Achille Castiglioni, 1992
Flos
H 134/178/197 cm

Also studied in Milan until 1936. Amongst other objects he designed audio-visual environments, lamps and electrical appliances. After 1952 he worked on his own, for companies that included the Italian broadcasting service, Olivetti, Brionvega and Fiat.

Ebenfalls Studium in Mailand bis 1936. Schuf u. a. audiovisuelle Environments, Lampen und Elektrogeräte. Arbeitete seit 1952 selbständig, u. a. für den italienischen Rundfunk, Olivetti, Brionvega, Fiat.

Etudie lui aussi l'architecture à Milan jusqu'en 1936. A créé, entre autres, des environnements audiovisuels, des lampes et des appareils électriques. A partir de 1952, travaille à son compte pour la radio italienne, Olivetti, Brionvega, Fiat, etc.

Livio Castiglioni
(*1911–1979)

Graduate of the Milan Polytechnic (1962). Works primarily in the fields of graphic and exhibition design. In 1986 he designed the Futurism exhibition at the Palazzo Grassi in Venice. He is a member of the Gregotti Associati studio. Artistic director of B&B Italia since 1982. He has designed furniture and lamps for Poltrona Frau and Fontana Arte.

Absolvent des Polytechnikums in Mailand (1962). Befaßt sich überwiegend mit Grafik- und Ausstellungsdesign. 1986 gestaltete er die Futurismus-Ausstellung im Palazzo Grassi in Venedig. Mitglied des Studios Gregotti Associati. Seit 1982 künstlerischer Leiter bei B&B Italia. Möbel- und Lampenentwürfe für Poltrona Frau und Fontana Arte.

Diplômé de l'Ecole polytechnique de Milan (1962). Se consacre notamment au design graphique et d'expositions. Aménage en 1986 l'exposition sur le futurisme au Palazzo Grassi de Venise. Membre du Studio Gregotti Associati. Depuis 1982, directeur artistique chez B&B Italia. Créations de meubles et de luminaires pour Poltrona Frau et Fontana Arte.

Pierluigi Cerri
(*1939)

Studied in Grenoble and Turin. In 1921 he opened a studio in which he worked on glass – a material that is central to his work. He founded Fontana Arte – the artistic branch of the Fontana company – with Luigi Fontana in 1933. At this early stage Fontana Arte concentrated on the production of furniture, basic utensils and glass objects. Chiesa's crystal table »2633« (design 1933) is a modern classic that is still in production.

Studium in Grenoble und Turin. 1921 Eröffnung einer Werkstatt für Verarbeitung von Glas, dem Material, das im Mittelpunkt seiner Arbeit steht. 1933 mit Luigi Fontana Gründung der Firma Fontana Arte, des künstlerischen Zweiges des Unternehmens Fontana. Fontana Arte konzentrierte sich zunächst auf die Herstellung von Möbeln, Gebrauchsgegenständen und Objekten aus Glas. Chiesas Kristalltisch »2633« (Entwurf 1933) gehört zu den modernen Klassikern, die noch produziert werden.

Etudes à Grenoble et à Turin. Ouvre, en 1921, un atelier pour la transformation du verre, matériau qui prédomine dans ses ouvrages. Fonde, en 1933, avec Luigi Fontana la firme Fontana Arte, succursale artistique de l'entreprise Fontana. Fontana Arte se concentre en premier lieu sur la fabrication de meubles, d'objets usuels et d'objets en verre. La table en cristal «2633», créée en 1933 par Chiesa, compte parmi les classiques modernes qui sont encore fabriqués de nos jours.

Pietro Chiesa
(*1892–1948)

Trained as a technician. Specialized in lamp designs. He worked for Artemide for seven years and has had his own company since 1978. His most famous design (with M. de André) is the »Daphine« lamp for Lumina.

Ausbildung zum Techniker. Spezialisiert auf Lampenentwürfe. Zunächst sieben Jahre lang für Artemide tätig, seit 1978 eigenes Unternehmen. Bekanntester Entwurf Lampe »Daphine« für Lumina mit M. de André.

Formation de technicien. Se spécialise dans les lampes. Travaille d'abord sept ans pour Artemide. Possède sa propre entreprise depuis 1978. Sa création la plus célèbre est la lampe «Daphine» réalisée pour Lumina avec M. de André.

Tomasso Cimini
(*1947)

Studied at the Milan Polytechnic until 1975. Active in furniture and industrial design since 1972, he has worked with Paolo Nava since 1973 and established his own studio in 1981. Amongst the companies he has worked for are Flexform, B&B Italia (his work here included its sofa system »Sity«), and Kartell. Since 1987 he has worked with the American architect Terry Dwan in their studio Citterio-Dawn. Commissions for interior design include Esprit stores.

Bis 1975 Studium am Mailänder Polytechnikum. Seit 1972 im Möbel- und Industriedesign tätig, seit 1973 Zusammenarbeit mit Paolo Nava. 1981 Gründung eines eigenen Studios. Arbeiten u. a. für Flexform, B&B Italia (u.a. Sofasystem »Sity«), Kartell. Seit 1987 Zusammenarbeit mit dem amerikanischen Architekten Terry Dwan im gemeinsamen Studio Citterio-Dwan. Aufträge für Innenausstattung u. a. für Esprit-Läden.

Etudes à l'Ecole polytechnique de Milan jusqu'en 1975. Travaille dans le design industriel et le design des meubles depuis 1972 et collabore avec Paolo Nava depuis 1973. Crée son propre studio en 1981. Travaux pour Flexform, B&B Italia (entre autres, canapé «Sity» à modulation variable), Kartell, etc. Depuis 1987, travaille avec l'architecte américain Terry Dwan dans leur studio Citterio Dwan. Commandes de décorations intérieures, entre autres pour les boutiques Esprit.

Antonio Citterio
(*1950)

Technical director of the Kartell company since it was founded in 1949. He designed many of the company's first plastic objects, such as household appliances, dish racks and plastic dishes. These designs were awarded the Compasso d'Oro in 1955, 1957, 1959, 1960.

Technischer Direktor der Firma Kartell seit deren Gründung 1949. Entwarf selbst viele der frühen Kunststoffobjekte des Hauses wie Haushaltsgeräte, Geschirrkörbe und Kunststoffgeschirr. Dafür 1955, 1957, 1959, 1960 mit dem Compasso d'Oro ausgezeichnet.

Directeur technique de Kartell depuis la fondation de la firme en 1949. Conçoit un grand nombre des premiers objets en matière plastique pour la maison: appareils électroménagers, égouttoirs et vaisselle en matière plastique. Reçoit le Compasso d'Oro en 1955, 1957, 1959 et 1960.

Gino Colombini
(*1915)

Studied in Milan at the Brera Academy of Art and the Polytechnic. In 1961 he turned away from sculpture and painting and opened a design studio in Milan. His well-known furniture designs included plastic chairs for the Kartell company, tables, lamps, and objects.

Studium an der Mailänder Kunstakademie Brera und am Polytechnikum. Wandte sich 1961 von Bildhauerei und Malerei ab und eröffnete ein Designstudio in Mailand. Bekannte Möbelentwürfe, u.a. Kunststoffstühle für die Firma Kartell, Tische, Lampen und andere Objekte.

Etudes à l'Académie des Beaux-Arts Brera et à l'Ecole polytechnique de Milan. Abandonne, en 1961, la sculpture et la peinture et ouvre un studio de design à Milan. Créations de meubles comprenant des chaises en plastique pour Kartell, des tables, des lampes et des objets.

Cesare »Joe« Colombo
(1930–1971)

Studied architecture in Turin. He built the Alpine Stadium (1985) and Automobile Museum (1987) in Turin. Designs for Artemide, Driade and Sawaya & Moroni.

Studium der Architektur in Turin. Baute zunächst das Alpenstadion (1985) und Automobilmuseum (1987) in Turin. Arbeitet für Artemide, Driade und Sawaya & Moroni.

Etudes d'architecture à Turin. A construit à Turin le stade des Alpes (1985) et le musée de l'automobile (1987). Travaille pour Artemide, Driade et Sawaya & Moroni.

Toni Cordero

Studied mechanical engineering at the Turin Polytechnic and was then the technical director at an airplane factory. In 1926 he founded his own company, where he developed helicopters according to Leonardo da Vinci's designs. In 1930 they achieved record flying heights and times. He began to work for the Piaggio company in Genoa in 1934. He designed airplane parts and helicopters but his greatest success was the development of the »Vespa«. Designed in 1945, it has been in production since 1946 and over 12 million have been sold.

Maschinenbaustudium am Polytechnikum in Turin, danach technischer Leiter einer Flugzeugfabrik. Nach dem Ersten Weltkrieg und 1926 Gründung eigener Firmen, unter anderem Entwicklung von Hubschraubern nach Leonardo da Vincis Entwürfen. 1930 Rekorde in Flughöhe und -dauer. 1934 Eintritt in die Firma Piaggio in Genua, Entwurf von Flugzeugteilen und Hubschraubern. Größter Erfolg war die Entwicklung der »Vespa« (Entwurf 1945, Produktion seit 1946), von der bis heute über 12 Millionen verkauft wurden.

Etudes de construction mécanique à l'Ecole polytechnique de Turin, puis directeur technique d'une usine aéronautique. Après la Première Guerre mondiale et après 1926, fondation de ses propres firmes et fabrication d'hélicoptères suivant les dessins de Léonard de Vinci. 1930, records d'altitude et de durée. 1934, entre dans la firme Piaggio à Gênes. Dessine des pièces d'avion et des hélicoptères. La «Vespa» fut son plus grand succès (création en 1945, production depuis 1946). Plus de 12 millions d'exemplaires ont été vendus jusqu'à ce jour.

Corradino d'Ascanio
(1891–1981)

Studied architecture in Florence until 1966. He was a founding member of Archizoom Associati in this year and Collettivo Tecnici Progettisti in 1975. Work includes architectural designs, townplanning projects, and restorations. Companies for which he has designed furniture include Cassina and Driade. He teaches at the University of Florence and in London. His work has been shown in numerous exhibitions on architecture and industrial design. His »Aeo« chair for Cassina has become a classic.

Bis 1966 Architekturstudium in Florenz. 1966 Mitbegründer von Archizoom Associati und 1975 des Collettivo Tecnici Progettisti. Architekturentwürfe, Urbanistikprojekte, Restaurierungen. Möbelentwürfe u.a. für die Firmen Cassina und Driade. Lehraufträge an den Universitäten in Florenz und in London. Teilnahme an zahlreichen Ausstellungen zu Architektur und Industriedesign. Ein Klassiker ist inzwischen sein Sessel »Aeo« für Cassina.

Etudes d'architecture à Florence jusqu'en 1966. Co fondateur d'Archizoom Associati en 1966 et de Collettivo Tecnici Progettisti en 1975. Projets d'architecture, d'urbanisme, restaurations, créations de meubles, entres autres, pour Cassina et Driade. Chargé de cours aux universités de Florence et de Londres. Participation à de nombreuses exposition sur l'architecture et le design industriel. Son fauteuil «Aeo» pour Cassina est devenu un classique.

Paolo Deganello
(*1940)

Studied architecture in Florence until 1975. After moving to Milan he took up contact with Andrea Branzi, Alessandro Mendini and Ettore Sottsass. Worked with Studio Alchimia and has been a member of the Memphis Group since 1981. Design consultant for Olivetti (office furniture, computers and banks) since 1979. Professor of industrial design at the University of Florence. Companies for which he designs include Kartell, Artemide and Arflex.

Bis 1975 Architekturstudium in Florenz. Nahm nach dem Umzug nach Mailand Kontakt mit Andrea Branzi, Alessandro Mendini und Ettore Sottsass auf. Mitarbeit am Studio Alchimia und seit 1981 Mitglied der Memphis-Gruppe. Seit 1979 Designberater für Olivetti für Büromöbelsysteme, Großrechner und Bankeinrichtungen. Lehrstuhl für Industriedesign an der Universität Florenz. Arbeitet u.a. für Kartell, Artemide, Arflex.

Etudes d'architecture à Florence jusqu'en 1975. Prend contact avec Andrea Branzi, Alessandro Mendini et Ettore Sottsass après s'être installé à Milan. Collaborateur au Studio Alchimia et, depuis 1981, membre du groupe Memphis. Depuis 1979, conseilleur en design chez Olivetti pour les meubles de bureau, les centres d'informatique et les équipements de banque. Professeur de design industriel à l'université de Florence. Travaille, entre autres, pour Kartell, Artemide, Arflex.

Michele de Lucchi
(*1951)

Graduates of the Milan Polytechnic. Have worked together since 1966 in the areas of architecture, town-planning, as well as furniture and product design. Inspired by the Pop Art movement, they attracted attention in the 1960s and 1970s with their provocative ironic designs, which included the inflatable plastic »Blow« chair (1967, Zanotta) and the »Joe« chair (1970, Poltronova), shaped to look like Joe Di Maggio's baseball mitt.

Absolventen des Polytechnikums in Mailand. Zusammenarbeit seit 1966 in den Bereichen Architektur, Stadtplanung, Möbel- und Produktdesign. Traten in den sechziger und siebziger Jahren durch von der Pop Art inspirierte, provozierend-ironische Entwürfe hervor wie den aufblasbaren Plastiksessel »Blow« (1967, Zanotta) oder den Sessel »Joe« (1970, Poltronova), dem Baseballhandschuh Joe Di Maggios nachgeformt.

Diplômés de l'Ecole polytechnique de Milan. Depuis 1966, collaboration dans les domaines de l'architecture, de l'urbanisme, du design des meubles et des objets. Se distinguent dans les années 60 et 70 avec leurs réalisations provocantes et ironiques qui s'inspirent du Pop Art. Citons ainsi le fauteuil en plastique gonflable «Blow» (1967, Zanotta) et le fauteuil «Joe» (1970) qui a la forme du gant de baseball de Joe Di Maggio.

Jonathan de Pas
(1932–1991),
Donato d'Urbino
(*1935),
Paolo Lomazzi
(*1936)

Graduate of the Milan Polytechnic, 1979. Companies he works for include Cappelini, Vistosi, and Fontana Arte. His most well-known design is his »Lipsia« programme of chairs and tables for Cappellini International.

Absolvent des Mailänder Polytechnikums (1979). Arbeitet u.a. für Cappellini, Vistosi und Fontana Arte. Bekanntester Entwurf seither: Stuhl- und Tischprogramm »Lipsia« für Cappellini International.

Diplômé de l'Ecole polytechnique de Milan (1979). Travaille, entre autres, pour Cappellini, Vistosi et Fontana Arte. Création la plus connue jusqu'à présent: programme chaises et tables «Lipsia» pour Cappellini International.

Rudi Dordoni

Studied architecture at the Milan Polytechnic. Have worked together since their graduation in 1926/27. Members of Gruppo 7 and Movimento Italiano per l'Architettura Razionale which represented rationalist architecture in Italy during the 1920s and 1930s. Worked for Olivetti in Ivrea, 1935–57. Designed the »Studio 42« portable typewriter in 1935. In 1933 they designed a radio for a competition held by Domus. The design was far ahead of its time but was never realized. Residential, commercial and industrial buildings in Milan, as well as a church.

Architekturstudium am Polytechnikum im Mailand. Seit dem Abschluß 1926/27 Zusammenarbeit. Mitglieder der Gruppo 7 und des Movimento Italiano per l'Architettura Razionale, die in den zwanziger, dreißiger Jahren in Italien die rationalistische Architektur vertraten. 1935–57 Tätigkeit für Olivetti in Ivrea. 1935 Entwurf der Reiseschreibmaschine »Studio 42«. 1933 zukunftsweisender Entwurf eines Radios für einen Domus-Wettbewerb, das nicht produziert wurde. In Mailand Wohn-, Büro- und Industriebauten sowie eine Kirche.

Etudes d'architecture à l'Ecole polytechnique de Milan. Collaboration depuis leur sortie de l'Ecole en 1926/27. Membres du Gruppo 7 et du Movimento Italiano per l'Architettura Razionale qui représentaient l'architecture rationaliste en Italie dans les années 20 et 30. 1955–57, travaillent pour Olivetti à Ivrea. 1935, créent la machine à écrire portative «Studio 42» pour un concours Domus. Elle ne fut pas fabriquée. Construisent des maisons d'habitation, des immeubles de bureaux et des bâtiments industriels de même qu'une église.

Luigi Figini
(*1903),
Gino Pollini
(*1903)

Studied at the Brera Art Academy in Milan. First designs in 1970. Met Vico Magistretti in 1975, who was an important influence on him. Moved to London in 1978. In 1979 he was one of the founding members of the Alias company whose objective is the continuation of functionalist design. Lamp designs for Artemide. Lives and works in Milan. Important pieces include the »Icaro« wall lamp and the »Apocalypse now« table.

Studium an der Kunstakademie Brera in Mailand. Seit 1970 erste Designentwürfe. 1975 Begegnung mit Vico Magistretti, von dem er wichtige Anregungen erhielt. Ließ sich 1978 in London nieder, 1979 Mitbegründer der Firma Alias, die sich der Fortführung funktionalistischen Designs verschrieben hat. Lampenentwürfe für Artemide. Lebt und arbeitet in Mailand. Wichtige Arbeiten: Wandlampe »Icaro« und Tisch »Apokalypse Now«.

Etudes à l'Académie des Beaux-Arts Brera de Milan. Se consacre au design depuis 1970. En 1975, rencontre Vico Magistretti dont les idées lui seront précieuses. S'installe à Londres en 1978. Cofondateur, en 1979, de la firme Alias qui se consacre au design fonctionnaliste. Créations de luminaires pour Artemide. Vit et travaille à Milan. Ouvrages principaux: applique «Icaro» et table «Apocalypse Now».

Carlo Forcolini
(*1947)

Painter, graphic artist, illustrator. Studied philosophy, painting, and sculpture but was essentially self-taught. During the 1950s he worked in close collaboration with Giò Ponti, whose furniture and interior furnishings he decorated with drawings (architectural and otherwise) in a trompe-l'œil-style. e.g. the rooms of the casino at San Remo, 1952. Later, he designed objects and furniture which were realized in his own workshop. There was a retrospective of his work in the Victoria and Albert Museum, London 1991/92. His work is being carried on by his son, Barnaba.

Maler, Grafiker, Illustrator. Studium der Philosophie, Malerei, Bildhauerei, blieb jedoch im wesentlichen Autodidakt. In den fünfziger Jahren enge Zusammenarbeit mit Giò Ponti, dessen Möbel und Innenausstattungen er mit Architektur- oder anderen Zeichnungen im Trompe-l'œil-Stil dekorierte, so 1952 in den Räumen des Casino von San Remo. Später eigene Objekt- und Möbelentwürfe, die er in einer eigenen Werkstatt realisierte. 1991/92 Retrospektive im Victoria and Albert Museum in London. Seine Arbeit wird von seinem Sohn Barnaba fortgeführt.

Peintre, dessinateur, illustrateur. Etudie la philosophie, la peinture et la sculpture, mais est surtout autodidacte. Dans les années 50, étroite collaboration avec Giò Ponti dont il décore les meubles et les aménagements intérieurs avec des dessins et des constructions en trompe-l'œil, comme dans les salles du casino de San Remo en 1952. Dessine plus tard ses propres objets et meubles qu'il fabrique dans son atelier. 1991/92, rétrospective au Victoria and Albert Museum de Londres. Son fils Barnaba poursuit son travail.

Piero Fornasetti
(1913–1988)

Graduate of the Milan Polytechnic (1953). Worked for Giò Ponti, 1952/54. Opened his own studio. Has designed for Bernini since 1956. His work reflects the company's tradition of placing high value on the excellent finishing of costly materials. He has also designed tables and chairs for Cassina, and lamps for Artemide. His »Boalum« lamp (with Livio Castiglioni), which was constructed out of synthetic materials, made design history.

Absolvent des Polytechnikums in Mailand (1953). 1952–54 tätig für Giò Ponti. Gründung eines eigenen Studios. Seit 1956 Entwürfe für Bernini im Sinne des Unternehmens, das Wert legt auf exzellente Verarbeitung wertvoller Materialien. Tisch- und Sesselentwürfe auch für Cassina, Lampen für Artemide. Designgeschichte gemacht hat seine gemeinsam mit Livio Castiglioni konzipierte Kunststofflampe »Boalum«.

Diplômé de l'Ecole polytechnique de Milan (1953). 1952–54, travaille pour Giò Ponti. Crée son propre studio. Depuis 1956, créations pour Bernini conformément à la philosophie de l'entreprise qui attache une grande importance à une transformation excellente des matériaux précieux. Tables et fauteuils pour Cassina, luminaires pour Artemide. Sa lampe «Boalum» en matière plastique, qui fut conçue avec Livio Castiglioni, est entrée dans l'histoire du design.

Gianfranco Frattini
(*1926)

An architectural group based in Turin that has been working together since 1965 in the areas of architecture, town planning, graphic and industrial design. Their famous »Sacco« chair (1969) received many awards. A sack made of either synthetic material or leather and filled with polyester balls, it is still manufactured by Zanotta and is included in many design collections.

In Turin ansässige Architektengruppe, die seit 1965 in den Bereichen Architektur, Städtebau, Grafik- und Industriedesign zusammenarbeitet. Berühmt wurde ihr Sessel »Sacco« (1969), ein vielprämierter, mit Polyesterkugeln gefüllter Kunststoff- oder Ledersack, der noch von Zanotta produziert wird und in Designsammlungen vertreten ist.

Groupe d'architectes établis à Turin. Depuis 1965, collaboration dans le domaine de l'architecture, de l'urbanisme, du design graphique et industriel. Leur fauteuil «Sacco» (1969), un «sac» en cuir ou en plastique rempli de billes en polyester, est devenu célèbre et a reçu plusieurs prix. Il est aujourd'hui encore fabriqué par Zanotta et figure dans plusieurs collections de design.

Piero Gatti
(*1940),
Cesare Paolini
(*1937),
Franco Teodoro
(*1939)

Starting as an engineer at Fiat in 1928, he first worked on airplane motors. Beginning in 1932, for the next fifty years he would work on the company's cars. His most famous designs are the »500A«, the so-called »Topolino« (1936) and the »500 Nuova« (1957), one of the most popular cars of the post-war era. He was also responsible for the Fiat models 124, 128 and 130.

Trat 1928 als Ingenieur bei Fiat ein, wo er sich zunächst mit Flugzeugmotoren beschäftigte. Seit 1932 widmete er seine Arbeit fünfzig Jahre lang den Autos des Unternehmens. Die bekanntesten Entwürfe sind der »500A«, der sogenannte »Topolino« (1936), und der »500 Nuova« (1957), eines der verbreitetsten Autos der Nachkriegszeit. Von ihm konzipiert wurden auch die Fiat-Modelle 124, 128 und 130.

Entre comme ingénieur chez Fiat en 1928 et travaille au début sur les moteurs d'avion. A partir de 1932, s'est consacré, pendant 50 ans, aux automobiles de l'entreprise. Ses créations les plus célèbres sont la «500 A», la «Topolino» (1936) et la «500 Nuova» (1957), l'une des voitures les plus répandues après la guerre. Il conçoit également les modèles 124, 128 et 130 de Fiat.

Dante Giacosa
(*1905)

Studied at the Milan Polytechnic and at the Scuola Superiore di Ingegneria, Rome. Together with Sergio Mazza, he founded Artemide in 1959. Initially, the company only manufactured lamps. President and principal owner of Memphis. 1981. Gismondi produced successful designs for Artemide and also commissioned the best designers for the company. He was professor of rocket technology at the Milan Polytechnic until 1984.

Studium am Polytechnikum Mailand und an der Scuola Superiore di Ingegneria, Rom. Gründete 1959 mit Sergio Mazza das Unternehmen Artemide, das zunächst nur Lampen herstellte. 1981 wurde er Präsident und Haupteigner von Memphis. Für Artemide fertigte Gismondi selbst erfolgreiche Entwürfe und beauftragte die besten Designer. Bis 1984 Professor für Raketentechnik am Mailänder Polytechnikum.

Etudes à l'Ecole polytechnique de Milan et à la Scuola Superiore di Ingegneria de Rome. En 1959, avec Sergio Mazza l'entreprise Artemide qui ne fabrique au départ que des luminaires. Devient, en 1981, président et propriétaire principal de Memphis. Ses propres créations pour Artemide connaissent un grand succès. Il passe également des commandes aux meilleurs designers. Jusqu'en 1984, professeur à l'Ecole polytechnique de Milan et enseigne la technique des fusées.

Ernesto Gismondi
(*1931)

One of the most versatile of Italian designers. After studying arts at the Academy of Fine Arts in Turin, he began to work for Fiat in 1955, became a designer for Carozzeria Bertone in 1959 and became the director of the Ghia design studio in 1965. Opened his own studio, Italdesign in 1968. It has worked on developing the Fiat models »Panda« and »Uno; the VW «Golf»; and the «Alfasud» for Alfa Romeo. His studio also designs sewing machines, furniture, clocks, noodles and for Nikon cameras.

Einer der vielseitigsten italienischen Designer. Zunächst Kunststudium an der Akademie der Schönen Künste in Turin, trat 1955 ins Unternehmen Fiat ein, ging 1959 als Designer zur Carozzeria Bertone und wurde 1965 Leiter des Ghia Designstudios. Gründete 1968 sein Studio Italdesign, das u.a. die Fiat-Modelle »Panda« und »Uno«, den VW »Golf« und den »Alfasud« für Alfa Romeo entwickelte. Daneben entwirft Italdesign Nähmaschinen, Möbel, Uhren, Nudeln oder Kameras für Nikon.

L'un des designers italiens aux talents multiples. Etudes d'art à l'Académie des Beaux-Arts de Turin, puis entre chez Fiat en 1955. Travaille comme designer à Carozzeria Bertone en 1959 et devient directeur du studio de design Ghia en 1965. Fonde, en 1968, son studio Italdesign qui réalise, entre autres, les modèles «Panda» et «Uno» pour Fiat, la «Golf» pour VW et l'«Alfasud» pour Alfa Romeo. Parallèlement, Italdesign se charge du design des machines à coudre, des meubles, des pendules, des pâtes et des appareils-photos pour Nikon.

Giorgio Giugiaro
(*1938)

Studied at the Polytechnic in Milan until 1952. Close collaboration with Lodovico Meneghetti and Giotto Stoppino, 1953–68. Founded Gregotti Associati with Pierluigi Cerri and Hiromichi Matsui, 1974. Editor of Casabella-Continuità and editor-in-chief of Edilizia Moderna, journals in which he published numerous theoretical writings. Professor of architecture at the University of Venice since 1971. Many other teaching positions. Has designed for Fontana Arte and B & B Italia.

Bis 1952 Studium am Polytechnikum in Mailand. Von 1953 bis 1968 enge Zusammenarbeit mit Lodovico Meneghetti und Giotto Stoppino. Gründete 1974 mit Pierluigi Cerri und Hiromichi Matsui Gregotti Associati. Redakteur bzw. Chefredakteur der Zeitschriften »Casabella-Continuità« und »Edilizia Moderna«, in denen er zahlreiche theoretische Schriften veröffentlicht. Seit 1971 Professor am Institut für Architektur an der Universität Venedig. Verschiedene andere Lehraufträge. Entwürfe u.a. für Fontana Arte, B&B Italia.

Etudes à l'Ecole polytechnique de Milan jusqu'en 1952. De 1953 à 1968, collaboration étroite avec Lodovico Meneghetti et Giotto Stoppino. Fonde, en 1974, Gregotti Associati avec Pierluigi Cerri et Hiromichi Matsui. Rédacteur et rédacteur en chef des revues «Casabella-Continuità» et «Edilizia Moderna», dans lesquelles il fait paraître de nombreux articles théoriques. Depuis 1971, professeur à l'Institut d'architecture de l'université de Venise. Plusieurs fois chargé de cours. Créations, entre autres, pour Fontana Arte et B&B Italia.

Vittorio Gregotti
(*1927)

Studied architecture in Florence and Milan. Drew comic strips at the beginning of his career. Works as a deign consultant for RAI, the Italian broadcasting service. Founded the AGO company 1984, designed discotheques, video projects and magazines. Represented in the Memphis collection since 1986. Presented his first collection – »Dinamic« – in 1987. Numerous furniture and industrial designs, including portable radios and televisions for manufacturers all over the world. One of the young design stars in Milan of whom much is expected.

Architekturstudium in Florenz und Mailand, zeichnete zunächst Comics. Arbeitet als Designberater für den staatlichen italienischen Rundfunk RAI. Gründete 1984 die Firma AGO, gestaltete Diskotheken, Videoprojekte und Zeitschriften. Seit 1986 in der Memphis-Kollektion vertreten. Stellte 1987 seine erste eigene Kollektion »Dinamic« vor. Zahlreiche Möbel- und Industrieentwürfe, u.a. für tragbare Radios und Fernseher für Hersteller in der ganzen Welt. Einer der jungen Designstars in Mailand, in die hohe Erwartungen gesetzt werden.

Etudes d'architecture à Florence et à Milan. Réalise tout d'abord des bandes dessinées. Travaille comme conseiller en design à la RAI, chaîne publique italienne de radiodiffusion. Fonde, en 1984, la firme AGO, réalise la décoration intérieure de discothèques et le design de vidéos et de revues. Est représenté dans la collection Memphis depuis 1986. Présente sa première collection «Dinamic» en 1987. Nombreux meubles et produits industriels, entre autres pour les fabricants de radios et de téléviseurs portables du monde entier. Fait partie des jeunes stars milanaises du design dont on attend encore beaucoup.

Massimo Iosa Ghini
(*1959)

King Miranda Associati, established in 1977, is one of Milan's most successful design studios. Originally from England, King studied at the Birmingham School of Art. He then went to Italy and began to work for Olivetti in 1965, where he developed the »Valentine« typewriter with Sottsass. Miranda is Spanish and studied in Seville. He first worked with King in Italy on the project »Unlimited Horizon«, a study of the reciprocal relationship between design and living-space. Later on there were many designs for furniture, lamps (Flos, Arteluce) and electric tools.

King Miranda Associati ist seit 1977 eines der erfolgreichsten Mailänder Designstudios. Der Engländer King studierte an der Birmingham School of Art, ging nach Italien und arbeitete ab 1965 für Olivetti, wo er mit Sottsass die Schreibmaschine »Valentine« entwickelte. Der Spanier Miranda studierte in Sevilla. Erste Zusammenarbeit mit King in Italien am Projekt »Unlimited Horizon«, einer Untersuchung über Wechselwirkung zwischen Design und Lebensraum. Später zahlreiche Entwürfe für Möbel, Lampen (Flos, Arteluce) und Elektrowerkzeuge.

Depuis 1977, le King Miranda Associati est l'un des studios de design milanais qui connaissent le plus de succès. L'Anglais King a étudié à la Birmingham School of Art. Après s'être installé en Italie, il a travaillé, à partir de 1965, chez Olivetti où il a réalisé avec Sottsass la machine à écrire «Valentine». L'Espagnol Miranda a étudié à Séville. Première collaboration avec King en Italie pour le projet «Unlimited Horizon», une étude sur l'interaction entre le design et l'espace vital. Plus tard, nombreuses créations de meubles, de luminaires (Flos, Arteluce) et d'outils électriques.

Perry A. King
(*1938),
Santiago Miranda
(*1947)

Trained as a carpenter, he has worked as an independent designer since 1965. After some eccentric furniture designs (including a glass chair), he has worked primarily as an interior designer for fashion houses such as Issey Miyake and the Seibu department stores in Japan. His designs for Italian manufacturers include the chest of drawers » Solaris« and »Side 1/2« for Cappellini.

Nach einer Tischlerlehre seit 1965 selbständig als Designer. Nach einigen exzentrischen Möbelentwürfen (ein Glassessel u.a.) vor allem Innenarchitektur für Modeunternehmen wie Issey Miyake und die Seibu-Kaufhäuser in Japan. Entwürfe für italienische Hersteller, u.a. die Kommoden »Solaris« und »Side 1/2« für Cappellini.

Formation d'ébéniste. Travaille depuis 1965 comme designer indépendant. Après avoir créé des meubles excentriques (entre autres, un fauteuil en verre), se consacre surtout à la décoration intérieure de maisons de mode comme Issey Miyake et les grands magasins Seibu au Japon. Créations pour des fabricants italiens, entre autres les commodes «Solaris» et «Side 1/2» pour Cappellini.

Shiro Kuramata
(1934–1991)

As is true of many Italian designers, he too studied at the Milan Polytechnic. Doctorate, 1945. He first worked for his father's architectural office before he opened his own studio in Milan. Architect, town-planner, designer and teacher. He has built cinemas, hotels, residential and commercial buildings. Furniture and lamp designs for Artemide, Gavina, Cassina, OLuce, De Padova. His most famous designs include the »Atollo« lamp (1977, OLuce) and the »Selene« chair (1968/69, Artemide).

Wie viele italienische Designer Studium am Polytechnikum Mailand mit Promotion (1945). Trat zunächst ins väterliche Architekturbüro ein, bevor er ein eigenes Studio in Mailand gründete. Architekt, Stadt-planer, Designer und Dozent. Baute Kinos, Hotels, Wohn- und Ge-schäftshäuser. Möbel- und Lampen-entwürfe für Artemide, Gavina, Cassina, OLuce, De Padova. Unter seinen bekanntesten Entwürfen die Lampe »Atollo« (1977, OLuce) und der Stuhl »Selene« (1968/69, Artemide).

Comme beaucoup d'autres desi-gners italiens, études à l'Ecole polytechnique de Milan (doctorat en 1945). Entre tout d'abord dans le cabinet d'architecte de son père, puis fonde son propre studio à Milan. Architecte, urbaniste, desi-gner et maître de conférences. Construit des cinémas, des hôtels, des maisons d'habitation et des locaux commerciaux. Créations de meubles et de luminaires pour Artemide, Gavina, Cassina, OLuce, De Padova. La lampe «Atollo» (1977, OLuce) et la chaise «Selene» (1968/69, Artemide) comptent parmi ses ouvrages les plus célèbres.

Studied at the Hochschule für Gestaltung in Ulm. Returned to Italy. Worked in Fiat's design centre under Dante Giacosa. First designs for the Fiat »127«. A year before his fatal car crash he developed the prototype of a city taxi for Fiat. His concept for the »Parentesi« lamp was completed by Achille Casti-glioni.

Studium an der Hochschule für Gestaltung in Ulm. 1965 Rückkehr nach Italien. Eintritt ins Design-zentrum von Fiat unter Dante Gia-cosa. Erste Entwürfe für den Fiat »127«. Entwickelte ein Jahr vor seinem tödlichen Autounfall für Fiat den Prototyp eines City-Taxis. Sein Konzept für die Lampe »Parentesi« wurde von Achille Castiglioni vollen-det.

Etudes à l'Ecole supérieure d'esthé-tique pratique d'Ulm. 1965, retour en Italie. Entre au centre de design de Fiat, sous la direction de Dante Giacosa. Premiers dessins pour la Fiat «127». Un an avant sa mort dans un accident de voiture, réalise pour Fiat le prototype d'un City Taxi. Son concept pour la lampe «Parentesi» est terminé par Achille Castiglioni.

Graduate of the Brera Academy of Arts in Milan (1956). Since 1952 has published a great deal on theory and on art. He designed for Danese and Driade since 1956. Developed designs for textiles and wall tiles, household appliances, toys and book covers, wrote children's books and a historical novel. Teaches at universities in Milan and Rome. His »Delfina« chair (1974, Driade) has now become a classic and was awarded the Compasso d'Oro.

Absolvent der Kunstakademie Brera in Mailand (1956). Seit 1952 zahl-reiche theoretische Veröffentlichun-gen, auch über Kunst. Seit 1956 Entwürfe für die Unternehmen Da-nese und Driade. Entwickelte Textil- und Wandfliesenentwürfe, Haus-haltsgeräte, Spielzeug und Buch-umschläge, schrieb Kinderbücher und einen historischen Roman. Lehrt an den Unversitäten Mailand und Rom. Sein Stuhl »Delfina« (1974, Driade), inzwischen ein Klassiker, erhielt den Compasso d'Oro.

Diplômé de l'Académie des Beaux-Arts Brera de Milan (1956). Depuis 1952, nombreuses publications théoriques, également sur l'art. Depuis 1956, réalisations pour les entreprises Danese et Driade. Crée des textiles, des carreaux muraux, des jouets et des couvertures de livres. A écrit des livres pour enfants et un roman historique. Enseigne aux universités de Milan et de Rome. Sa chaise «Delfina» (1974, Driade), qui est devenue un classi-que, a reçu le Compasso d'Oro.

Studied architecture in Lausanne until 1954. Has had his own studio in Milan since 1956. Lamp designs for Artemide, furniture designs for other manufacturers. Collaboration with Giuliana Gramigna in Studio SMC Architettura since 1961. Editor-in-chief of Ottagono, 1966–86.

Architekturstudium in Lausanne bis 1954. Seit 1956 eigenes Studio in Mailand. Lampenentwürfe für Arte-mide, Möbelentwürfe für andere Hersteller. Seit 1961 Zusammenar-beit mit Giuliana Gramigna im Studio SMC Architettura. 1966–86 Chefredakteur der Zeitschrift »Ottagono«.

Etudes d'architecture à Lausanne jusqu'en 1954. Possède son propre studio à Milan depuis 1956. Lumi-naires pour Artemide, meubles pour d'autres fabricants. Depuis 1961, collaboration avec Giuliana Gra-migna au studio SMC Architettura. 1966–86, rédacteur en chef de la revue «Ottagono».

Diploma in mechanical engineering, Milan Polytechnic, 1969. Assistant to the director of production at Magneti Marelli until 1973. Technical director at Kartell since 1973. Has developed the uses of both polyurethane and plastics for furniture. Freelance as a product and planning engineer since 1979. Worked for Alfa Romeo, 1981–85. Furniture and lamp designs for Alias and Luceplan since 1987.

1969 Diplom in Maschinenbau am Polytechnikum Mailand. Bis 1973 Assistent in der zentralen Pro-duktionsleitung bei Magneti Marelli. Ab 1973 technischer Leiter bei Kartell. Verantwortlich u.a. für die Entwicklung der Polyurethanver-arbeitung und die Produktion von Kunststoffmöbeln. Seit 1979 frei-beruflich als Produkt- und Pla-nungsingenieur. 1981–85 bei Alfa Romeo. Seit 1987 für Alias und Luceplan Möbel- und Lampen-entwürfe.

1969, diplôme de construction mécanique à l'Ecole polytechnique de Milan. Jusqu'en 1973, assistant du chef de production chez Magneti Marelli. A partir de 1973, directeur technique chez Kartell. Respon-sable, entre autres, des découvertes effectuées dans le traitement du polyuréthane et de la production de meubles en matière plastique. Depuis 1979, ingénieur indépendant pour les études de produit et de planification. 1981–85, chez Alfa Romeo. Depuis 1987, créations de meubles et de luminaires pour Alias et Luceplan.

Vico Magistretti
(*1920)

Pio Manzù
(1939–1969)

Enzo Mari
(*1932)

Sergio Mazza
(*1931)

Alberto Meda
(*1945)

Trained as an aeronautical engineer in Genoa. Founded the lamp manufacturing company Arteluce, 1939. During the Second World War he went into Swiss exile and subsequently rebuilt the company in Milan. He produced important designs in the 1940s and 1950s. Received the first Compasso d'Oro for his table lamp »559«, 1954. Arteluce is one of the companies that laid the foundations for modern Italian lamp design.

Zunächst Ausbildung zum Luftfahrtingenieur in Genua. Gründete 1939 seine Lampenfabrik Arteluce. Im Zweiten Weltkrieg Exil in der Schweiz, danach Wiederaufbau des Unternehmens in Mailand. Wichtige eigene Entwürfe in den vierziger und fünfziger Jahren. 1954 erster Compasso d'Oro für die Tischlampe »559«. Arteluce gehörte zu den Unternehmen, die das moderne italienische Lampendesign begründeten.

Tout d'abord, formation d'ingénieur aéronautique à Gênes. Fonde en 1939 son usine de lampes Arteluce. Exil en Suisse pendant la Seconde Guerre mondiale, puis reconstruction de l'entreprise à Milan. Créations personnelles importantes dans les années 40 et 50. En 1954, premier Compasso d'Oro pour la lampe de table «559». Arteluce est l'une des entreprises qui ont créé le design moderne des lampes italiennes.

Studied architecture at the Academy of Fine Arts in Venice until 1926. Active as an architect and designer since 1931. Glass designs for Venini, e.g. the »Tessuto« and »Battuto« series, 1933–47. He gained fame for his exhibition architecture and his careful restoration of palaces and museums, e.g. Castelvecchio Museum, Verona and the Ca'Foscari, Venice. Designed furniture primarily for Bernini and Simon International. For thirty years (beginning in 1942) he would act as adviser to the Biennale in Venice.

Bis 1926 Architekturstudium an der Akademie der schönen Künste, Venedig. Seit 1931 als Architekt und Designer tätig. 1933–47 Glasentwürfe für Venini, z.B. die Serien »Tessuto«, »Battuto«. Bekannt durch Ausstellungsarchitekturen und behutsame Restaurierungen von Palästen und Museen, z.B. Castelvecchio Museum, Verona, und der Ca'Foscari, Venedig. Möbelentwürfe vor allem für Bernini und Simon International. Ab 1942 war er 30 Jahre Berater für die Biennale in Venedig.

Etudes d'architecture à l'Académie des Beaux-Arts de Venise jusqu'en 1926. Travaille comme architecte et designer à partir de 1931. De 1933 à 1947, réalisation d'objets en verre pour Venini, comme les séries «Tessuto» et «Battuto». Célèbre par ses architectures d'expositions et ses restaurations soignées de palais et de musées, comme le musée Castelvecchio à Vérone et le Ca'Foscari à Venise. Réalisation de meubles notamment pour Bernini et Simon International. Pendant 30 ans, conseiller de la Biennale de Venise (à partir de 1942).

Carlo Scarpa's son and daughter-in-law. They both studied architecture in Venice until 1969. Have worked together since 1957. In the same year they produced their first designs for Venini. These were followed by furniture designs for Gavina, Cassina, and B&B, as well as lamp designs for Flos. They are committed to the restoration of old Venetian buildings.

Sohn und Schwiegertochter Carlo Scarpas. Beide Architekturstudium in Venedig bis 1969. Zusammenarbeit seit 1957. Im gleichen Jahr erste Entwürfe für Venini. Danach Möbelentwürfe für Gavina, Cassina, B&B, Lampen für Flos. Engagiert bei der der Restaurierung alter Häuser Venetiens.

Tobia (*1935) et Afra (*1937) Scarpa Fils et belle-fille de Carlo Scarpa. Tous deux, études d'architecture à Venise jusqu'en 1969. Collaboration depuis 1957. La même année, premières créations pour Venini. Puis création de meubles pour Gavina, Cassina, B&B, et de lampes pour Flos. Soutiennent la restauration des maisons anciennes de Vénétie.

Worked for Artemide in the 1960s. Important designs for furniture made of synthetic materials and for items of daily use.

In den sechziger Jahren für Artemide tätig. Wichtige Entwürfe für Kunststoffmöbel und -gebrauchsgegenstände.

Travaille pour Artemide dans les années 60. Réalisations importantes de meubles et d'objets usuels en matière plastique.

Active in Rome and Milan within different cultural spheres, from art and architecture to film and literature. In recent years has designed for Sawaya & Moroni. Post-Modern, nostalgic forms.

Tätig in verschiedenen Bereichen des kulturellen Lebens von Kunst über Architektur bis Film und Literatur in Rom und Mailand. In den letzten Jahren Entwürfe für Sawaya & Moroni. Postmoderne, nostalgische Formen.

Activités dans différents domaines de la vie culturelle à Rome et à Milan: art, architecture, cinéma, littérature, etc. Ces dernières années, créations pour Sawaya & Moroni. Formes postmodernes et nostalgiques.

Gino Sarfatti
(1912–1985)

Carlo Scarpa
(1906–1978)

Afra & Tobia Scarpa
(*1937, *1935)

Emma Schweinberger-Gismondi

Luigi Serafini
(*1949)

Born in Innsbruck, studied architecture in Turin until 1939. Active in many spheres, including painting, ceramics, architecture and industrial design. He worked in the Giuseppe Pagano office before opening his own studio in Milan in 1947. Responsible for the design of Olivetti office equipment since 1958 (»Tekne 3«, »Praxis 48«, »Valentine«, PC »M 20«). Exhibited in Studio Alchimia, founded the Memphis Group with other designers in 1981. In the early 1990s turned to archaic forms and classic materials.

In Innsbruck geboren, bis 1939 Architekturstudium in Turin. Tätig in vielen Bereichen von Malerei über Keramik, von Architektur bis zum Industriedesign. Zunächst im Büro von Giuseppe Pagano tätig, bevor er 1947 in Mailand ein eigenes Studio eröffnete. Seit 1958 zuständig für die Gestaltung von Olivetti-Büromaschinen (»Tekne 3«, »Praxis 48«, »Valentine«, PC »M 20«.). Stellte im Studio Alchimia aus, gründete 1981 mit anderen Designern die Gruppe Memphis. Anfang der neunziger Jahre Hinwendung zu archaischen Formen und klassischen Materialien.

Né à Innsbruck, études d'architecture à Turin jusqu'en 1939. Activités dans plusieurs domaines, allant de la peinture au design industriel en passant par la céramique et l'architecture. Travaille d'abord à l'agence de Giuseppe Pagano avant d'ouvrir son propre studio à Milan en 1947. Depuis 1958, responsable de l'aspect esthétique des machines de bureau Olivetti («Tekne 3», «Praxis 48», «Valentine», PC «M 20»). A exposé ses créations au studio Alchimia. Fonde en 1981 le groupe Memphis avec d'autres designers. Au début des années 90, se tourne vers les formes archaïques et les matériaux classiques.

Studied architecture in England. Consultant to Olivetti, 1970. Worked with Sottsass on the design of computer systems. Member of the Memphis Group. Furniture and lamp designs.

Architekturstudium in England. 1970 als Berater zu Olivetti. Zusammenarbeit mit Sottsass an der Entwicklung von Computersystemen. Mitglied der Memphis-Gruppe. Möbel- und Lampenentwürfe.

Etudes d'architecture en Angleterre. A partir de 1970, conseiller chez Olivetti. Collaboration avec Sottsass pour la réalisation d'ordinateurs. Membre du groupe Memphis. Création de meubles et de luminaires.

Studied architecture in Milan and Venice. Worked with Ernesto N. Rogers for 25 years. Became a partner of Vittorio Gregotti and Lodovicio Meneghetti in Studio Architetti Associati in 1953. Opened his own studio for architectural, furniture and above all industrial design in 1968. Designed objects made of plastics for the Kartell company. Has worked closely with Lodovicio Acerbis since 1976 and designs furniture with him for his company. President of ADI, 1982–85. Examples of his work can be found in important museums.

Architekturstudium in Mailand und Venedig. 25jährige Zusammenarbeit mit Ernesto N. Rogers. Von 1953 an Partner im Studio Architetti Associati mit Vittorio Gregotti und Lodovico Meneghetti. Seit 1968 eigenes Studio für Architektur, Möbel und vor allem Industriedesign. Entwürfe für Kunststoffobjekte der Firma Kartell. Seit 1976 enge Zusammenarbeit mit Lodovico Acerbis, mit dem er gemeinsam für dessen Unternehmen Möbel entwirft. 1982–85 ADI-Präsident. Seine Arbeiten sind in wichtigen Museen vertreten.

Etudes d'architecture à Milan et à Venise. 25 années de collaboration avec Ernesto N. Rogers. A partir de 1953, partenaire associé du studio Architetti Associati avec Vittorio Gregotti et Lodovico Meneghetti. Depuis 1968, possède son propre studio qui se consacre à l'architecture, aux meubles et surtout au design industriel. Création d'objets en matière plastique pour la firme Kartell. Depuis 1976, étroite collaboration avec Lodovico Acerbis et réalisation de meubles pour l'entreprise de ce dernier. 1982–85, président de l'ADI. Ouvrages dans de nombreux musées.

Founded in Florence in December 1966 by several young designers. Designs for buildings and objects. Participated in the foundation of Global Tools in 1972. The Superstudio work is considered to belong to the so-called radical or anti-design movement. The group existed until 1978. Its most famous design, which has now become a classic, is the »Quaderna« table system, with its laminated, latticed surface of synthetic material.

Im Dezember 1966 von einigen jungen Designern in Florenz gegründet. Architektur- und Designentwürfe. 1972 beteiligt an der Gründung von Global Tools. Die Entwürfe von Superstudio zählen zum sogenannten radikalen oder Anti-Design. Die Gruppe bestand bis 1978. Bekanntester und inzwischen klassischer Entwurf das mit kariertem Kunststofflaminat bezogene Tischsystem »Quaderna«.

Créé en décembre 1966 par quelques jeunes designers. Réalisations dans le domaine de l'architecture et du design. Participation à la fondation de Global Tools en 1972. Les créations de Superstudio font partie du design radical ou anti-design. Existence du groupe jusqu'en 1978. Réalisation la plus célèbre et comptant désormais parmi les classiques: ensemble de tables «Quaderna» avec un revêtement en aggloméré plastique à carreaux.

Studied architecture at the Milan Polytechnic until 1926. Participated in founding Gruppo 7, an association of rationalist architects that also included Luigi Figini and Gino Pollini. His major work is the Fascist party's Casa del Fascio in Como, 1934–36. (It is known today as the Casa del Populo). He designed tubular steel chairs for its interior – including »Follia« and »Lariana« – which are once again in production. Upon his return to Italy he died from the effects of a nervous breakdown that he had suffered on the Russian front.

Bis 1926 Studium der Architektur am Polytechnikum Mailand. Beteiligt an der Gründung der Gruppo 7, einer Vereinigung rationalistischer Architekten, zu denen auch Luigi Figini und Gino Pollini gehörten. Sein Hauptwerk, die Casa del Fascio der Faschistischen Partei in Como, heute Casa del Populo, entstand von 1934 bis 1936. Für die Inneneinrichtung entwarf er Stahlrohrsessel und -stühle, darunter »Follia« und »Lariana«, die wieder hergestellt werden. Starb, nach Italien zurückgekehrt, an den Folgen eines Nervenzusammenbruchs an der russischen Front.

Etudes d'architecture à l'Ecole polytechnique de Milan jusqu'en 1926. Participe à la création du Gruppo 7, association d'architectes rationalistes comprenant Luigi Figini et Gino Pollini. De 1934 à 1936, réalise son œuvre principale, la Casa del Fascio du parti fasciste à Côme, aujourd'hui Casa del Populo. Dessine pour l'aménagement intérieur les fauteuils et chaises en tubes d'acier, dont «Follia» et «Lariana» qui sont de nouveau fabriqués aujourd'hui. Après son retour en Italie, décède des suites d'une dépression nerveuse dont il avait souffert sur le front russe.

Ettore Sottsass
(*1917)

George James Sowden
(*1942)

Giotto Stoppino
(*1926)

Superstudio

Giuseppe Terragni
(1904–1943)

Studied architecture in Milan and also studied at the Oskar Kokoschka-Akademie in Salzburg. He was a partner at Sottsass Associati until 1984 and a founding member of the Memphis group. Has had his own studio for architecture and graphic design in Milan since 1984. Professor at the Hochschule für angewandte Kunst in Vienna since 1982. He teaches and lectures at many institutions. His objects – particularly his ceramic series – can be found in many important art and design musems, including the Victoria and Albert Museum in London.

Architekturstudium in Florenz und Besuch der Oskar-Kokoschka-Akademie in Salzburg. Bis 1984 Partner bei Sottsass Associati und Mitbegründer der Memphis-Gruppe. Seit 1984 eigenes Studio in Mailand für Architektur, Produkt- und Grafikdesign. Seit 1982 Professor an der Hochschule für angewandte Kunst in Wien, Lehr- und Vortragstätigkeit an vielen Institutionen. Seine Objekte – vor allem seine Keramikserien – befinden sich in wichtigen Kunst- und Designmuseen, u. a. dem Victoria and Albert Museum, London.

Etudie l'architecture à Florence et fréquente l'Académie Oskar Kokoschka à Salzbourg. Jusqu'en 1984, partenaire chez Sottsass Associati et cofondateur du groupe Memphis. Depuis 1984, possède son propre studio à Milan qui travaille dans le domaine de l'architecture, du design des produits et du design graphique. Depuis 1982, professeur à la Hochschule für angewandte Kunst à Vienne. Cours et conférences dans de nombreuses institutions. Ses objets – notamment ses séries de céramiques – figurent dans d'importants musées des beaux-arts et du design, entre autres au Victoria and Albert Museum de Londres.

Matteo Thun
(*1952)

Studied architecture in Venice until 1948 and then studied at the Harvard School of Design. He founded the Studio Architetti Vale with his sister in Udine. Active as an architect and town planner in northern Italy, particularly in Udine. Has designed kitchen and household appliances. Has specialized in schedule indicators for train stations and airports and in clocks. His desk clock »Cifra 3« was an international success.

Bis 1948 Architekturstudium in Venedig, danach an der Harvard School of Design, Cambridge (Mass.). Gründete mit seiner Schwester das Studio Architetti Vale in Udine. Tätig als Architekt und Stadtplaner in Norditalien, vor allem in Udine, entwarf Küchen und Haushaltsgeräte. Spezialisiert auf Fahrplananzeiger für Bahnhöfe und Flughäfen sowie Uhren. Ein Welterfolg wurde seine Schreibtischuhr »Cifra 3«.

Etudes d'architecture à Venise jusqu'en 1948, puis études à la Harvard School of Design, Cambridge (Mass.). Fonde avec sa sœur le studio Architetti Vale à Udine. Travaille comme architecte et urbaniste dans le Nord de l'Italie, en particulier à Udine. Réalise des utensiles de cuisine et des appareils ménagers. Spécialisé dans les télépancartages des gares et des aéroports ainsi que dans les pendules. Sa pendule de bureau «Cifra 3» a connu un succès mondial.

Gino Valle
(*1923)

Studied law in Milan. Together with Giacomo Cappelin, Andrea Rioda and Vittorio Zecchin, he founded a company for the production of glass objects in Venice in 1921. The company made use of traditional Venetian methods, but also developed new techniques which, from the very beginning, set Venini glass apart from the usual Murano products. The coloured objects were shown for the first time in 1923 at the Biennale in Monza, the predecessor of the Milan Triennale. In 1925 Venini took over the company as sole owner. Famous artists, architects and designers worked for Venini, and he himself also designed pieces. After his death the company was headed by his widow and his son-in-law, Ludovico de Santillana.

Jurastudium in Mailand. Gründete 1921 mit Giacomo Cappelin, Andrea Rioda und Vittorio Zecchin in Venedig eine Gesellschaft zur Herstellung von Glasobjekten. Das Unternehmen griff alte venezianische Verarbeitungstechniken auf, entwickelte aber auch neue, die das Venini-Glas von Anfang an von den üblichen Murano-Produkten unterschied. Auf der Biennale in Monza, der Vorläuferin der Triennale von Mailand, waren die farbigen Objekte 1923 erstmals zu sehen. 1925 übernahm Venini das Unternehmen als Alleininhaber. Berühmte Künstler, Architekten und Designer wirkten für Venini, der auch selbst Entwürfe anfertigte. Nach seinem Tode übernahmen seine Witwe und sein Schwiegersohn Ludovico de Santillana die Geschäftsführung.

Etudes de droit à Milan. En 1921, fonde à Venise avec Giacomo Cappelin, Andrea Rioda et Vittorio Zecchin une entreprise pour la fabrication d'objets en verre. Cette entreprise reprend d'anciennes techniques vénitiennes de transformation du verre, mais élabore également de nouvelles techniques de sorte que les objets en verre de Venini se distinguent dès le début des autres produits Murano. Les objets de couleur sont vus pour la première fois en 1923, lors de la Biennale de Monza, précurseur de la Triennale de Milan. En 1925, Venini devient l'unique propriétaire de l'entreprise. Des artistes, des architectes et des designers célèbres ont travaillé pour Venini qui a réalisé aussi ses propres objets. Après sa mort, sa femme et son gendre, Ludovico de Santillana, ont repris la gestion de son entreprise.

Paolo Venini
(1895–1959)

Studied architecture at the University of Florence. Has worked for Sottsass Associati since 1980. Designs furniture and glasses. Has also designed for the Memphis collections.

Architekturstudium an der Universität Florenz. Seit 1980 bei Sottsass Associati tätig. Entwirft Möbel und Gläser. Entwürfe auch für die Memphis-Kollektionen.

Etudes d'architecture à l'université de Florence. Travaille chez Sottsass Associati depuis 1980. Crée des meubles et des verres. Réalisations également pour les collections Memphis.

Marco Zanini
(*1954)

Graduated in 1939 from the Milan Polytechnic after studying architecture. Freelance architect and designer since 1945. Has worked for Olivetti in Buenos Aires and Sao Paulo as well as for Necchi in Pavia. He is one of the most important representatives of the second generation of 20th century Italian designers. After the end of the war he was editor of the journals Domus and Casabella-Continuità. Pioneering furniture designs in the 1950s; radios and televisions with Richard Sapper for Brionvega in the 1960s. Professor at the Milan Polytechnic.

1939 Absolvent des Polytechnikums Mailand nach Architekturstudium. Seit 1945 als freier Architekt und Designer tätig, u. a. für Olivetti in Buenos Aires und Sao Paulo sowie für Necchi in Pavia. Einer der wichtigsten Vertreter der zweiten Generation italienischer Designer des 20. Jahrhunderts. Nach Kriegsende Redakteur der Zeitschriften »Domus« und »Casabella-Continuità«. In den fünfziger Jahren wegweisende Möbelentwürfe, in den sechziger Jahren gemeinsam mit Richard Sapper Radios und Fernseher für Brionvega. Professor am Mailänder Polytechnikum.

Diplômé de l'Ecole polytechnique de Milan (1939) après des études d'architecture. Travaille depuis 1945 comme architecte et designer indépendant, entres autres, pour Olivetti à Buenos Aires et Sao Paulo et pour Necchi à Pavia. Est l'un des principaux représentants de la deuxième génération de designers italiens du XXᵉ siècle. Après la guerre, rédacteur des revues «Domus» et «Casabella-Continuità». Dans les années 50, création de meubles d'avant-garde; dans les années 60, réalisation de radios et de téléviseurs pour Brionvega avec Richard Sapper. Professeur à l'Ecole polytechnique de Milan.

Marco Zanuso
(*1916)

Abaco
Via Grialba 8
I-33028 Tolmezzo
Fax 0432-952235 (UD)

Acerbis International
Via Brusaporto 31
I-24068 Seriate (BG)
Fax 035-291454

Studio Alchimia
Corso San Gottardo 15
I-20136 Milano
Fax 011-2624046 (TO)

Alessi e Officina Alessi
I-28023 Crusinallo
Fax 0323-866127

Alfa Romeo
Centro Documentazione Storica
Viale Alfa Romeo
I-20020 Arese (MI)
Fax 002-93391

Alias
Via Leonardo da Vinci 29
I-24064 Grumello del Monte (BG)
Fax 035-440996

Anthologie Quartett
Schloß Huennefeld
D-49152 Bad Essen
Fax 005472-4348

Arflex
Via Monte Rosa 27
I-20051 Limbiate (MI)
Fax 02-9963933

Arteluce
Divisione della Flos
Via Angelos Faini 2
I-25073 Bovezzo (BS)
Fax 030-2711578

Artemide
Via Brughiera
I-20010 Pregnana Milanese (MI)
Fax 02-935-90496

B & B Italia
Strada Provinciale 32
I-22060 Novedrate (CO)
Fax 031-791592

Bernini
Via Fiume 17
I-20048 Carate Brianza (MI)
Fax 0362-990429

Bieffeplast
Via Pelosa 78
I-35030 Caselle di Selvazzano (PD)
Fax 049-635323

Bilumen
Via Salomone 41
I-20138 Milano
Fax 02-504039

Vittorio Bonacina & C
Via Madonnina 12
I-22040 Lurago d'Erba (CO)
Fax 031-699215

BRF
Loc S. Marziale
I-53034 Colle Val d'Elsa (SI)
Fax 0577-929648

Brionvega
Via Pordenone 8
I-20132 Milano
Fax 02-92108036

Cappellini
Via Marconi 35
I-22060 Arioso
Fax 031-763333/763322

Cassina
Via L. Vusnelli 1
I-20036 Meda (MI)
Fax 0362-342246/340959

Cleto Munari Design Associati
Via Generale Chinotto 3
I-36100 Vicenza
Fax 0444-542926

Bruno Danese
Via Pelizza da Volpedo 46/A
I-20092 Cinisello Balsamo (MI)
Fax 02-66016044

De Padova
Corso Venezia 14
I-20121 Milano
Fax 02-325442

Design Gallery Milano
Via Manzoni 46
I-20121 Milano
Fax 02-784082

Driade
Via Padana Inferiore 12
I-29012 Fossadello di Caorso (PC)
Fax 0523-822628

Fiat
Corso Marconi 20
I-10125 Torino
0039-11-6663408/6663798

Flexform
Via Einaudi 23/25
I-20036 Meda
Fax 0362-73055

Flos
Via Angelo Faini 2
I-25073 Bovezzo (BS)
Fax 03-02711578

Fontana Arte
Via Alzaia Trieste 49
I-20094 Corsico (MI)
Fax 02-4478135

Gufram
Via Francetti 27
I-10070 Bellengero (TO)
Fax 0123-346718

Hop-Là
Via Manzoni 11
I-20121 Milano
Fax 02-86464831/72022588

ICM (Industrie Casalinghi Mori)
Via Don Minzoni 1
I-25066 Lumezzane di Pieve (BS)
Fax 030-871450

Interflex
Chiara Costariol
Via Gusti 26
I-20154 Milano
Fax 02-33106747

Lamborghini
Via le F. Cassani 15
I-24047 Treviglio
Fax 0363-421638

Lancia
Via Vincenzo Lancia 27
I-10141 Torino
Fax 011-6853584

La Pavoni
Via Privata Gorizia 7
I-20098 San Giuliano Milanese (MI)
Fax 02-98241541

Longoni
Via Novara 5
I-22063 Cantù (CO)
Fax 031-713458

Luceplan
Via E. T. Moneta 44/46
I-20161 Milano
Fax 02-66203400

Lumina Italia
Via Casorezzo 63
I-200010 Arluno
Fax 02-90376528

Marcatrè
Via Sant'Andrea 3
I-20020 Misinto
Fax 02-96329038

Producers

Hersteller

Fabricants

Memphis
Via Olivetti 9
I-20010 Pregnana Milanese (MI)
Fax 02-93591202

Molteni & C.
Via Rossini 50
I-20034 Giussano
Fax 0362-852337

Moroso
Via Nazionale 60
I-33010 Cavalicco (UD)
0039-432-570761

Necchi
Viale della Republica 38
I-27100 Pavia
Fax 0382-514211

Olivetti
Via Porlezza 16
I-20123 Milano
Fax 02-76002291

OLuce
Via Cavour 52
I-20098 San Giuliano Milanese
(MI)
Fax 02-98490779

Piaggio
Corso Sempione 43
I-20145 Milano
Fax 02-33104581

Poltrona Frau
Strada Statale
I-62029 Tolentino (MC)
Fax 0733-971600

Poltronova
Via Provinciale Pratese 23
I-51037 Montale (PT)
Fax 0574-711251

Rimadesio
Via Bramante 9
I-20154 Milano
Fax 02-3490928

Sabattini Argenteria
Via Don Capiaghi 2
I-22070 Bregnano
Fax 031-773386

Saporiti Italia
Via Gallarate 23
I-21010 Besnate
Fax 0331-274125

Sawaya & Moroni
Via Manzoni 11
I-20121 Milano
Fax 02-86464831/ 72022588

S.I.D.I. (Società Italiana Disegno Industriale)
Via le Piave 3
I-20129 Milano
Fax 02-781677

Snaidero
Viale Europa Unita 9
I-33030 Majano (UD)
Fax 0432-952218/ 952235

Solari Udine
Via Gino Pieri 29
I-33100 Udine
Fax 0432-480160

Stilnovo
Via Borromini 12
I-20020 Lainate
Fax 02-9371074

Tecno
Via Bigli 22
I-20121 Milano
Fax 02-784484

Up & Up
Via Acquale 3
I-54100 Massa
Fax 0585-832038

Venini
Fondamente Vetrai 50
I-30100 Murano/Venezia
Fax 041-739369

Zani & Zani
Via del Porto 51/53
I-25088 Toscolano (BS)
Fax 0365-644281

Zanotta
Via Vittorio Veneto 57
I-20054 Nova Milanese (MI)
Fax 0362-451038

Zanussi
Corso Lino Zanussi 30
I-33080 Porcia (PN)
Fax 0434-396045

Zeus Noto
Via Vigevano 8
I-20144 Milano
Fax 02-89401142

Index

Photographic Credits

Bildnachweis

Crédits photographiques